THE GODS OF WAR

"Stillman's Gym" *(Holiday,* September 1947*)*

THE GODS OF WAR

Boxing Essays by
Springs Toledo

Published by Tora Book Publishing
ISBN 978-0-9543924-5-1

Cover Design by CJ McDaniel of Adazing Design with Springs Toledo © 2013

Cover photograph: Archie Moore at war with Rocky Marciano for the heavyweight crown, September 21, 1955 (photographer Yale Joel, Getty Images)

For Joe

Contents

Out of the Past

THE GODS OF WAR

Introduction

The Sweet Science, like an old rap or the memory of love, follows its victim everywhere. —A.J. Liebling

A well-fed and well-fêted writer for *The New Yorker* once considered turning his back on a favorite topic of his youth. During a train ride to Indianapolis to cover a heavyweight title bout in 1959, A.J. Liebling's affections rekindled. "I felt," he said, "the elation of a man who said a lot of hard things about a woman and is now on his way to make up."

As seedy as boxing was, is, and ever shall be, the writer could never leave it behind. He could never quite get it off his mind. Frankie Jerome couldn't either. After collapsing in the twelfth round during a bout at Madison Square Garden, his seconds carried him out of the ring, wrapped him in an overcoat, and brought him to Bellevue Hospital. Trainer Whitey Bimstein was there. "He died in my arms," he told Liebling, "slipping punches."

One of the last things that Liebling wrote was a reminiscence called "Paysage De Crepuscule," and even then a forgotten fighter from his youth jabbed his way onto a page. On December 28, 1963, it was the writer's turn to die. His editor walked into Liebling's office that day, and there, among stacks of books, newspapers, and lithographs was a drawing of old-time champion Bob Fitzsimmons. It was hanging on the wall at an odd angle as if it had been there a long time.

Thrice married, Liebling was never lucky in love. His first wife was a schizophrenic, the second a spendthrift, and the third an alcoholic. Perhaps he was prone to bad passion like any other perennial optimist who knew how to squint. Aren't we all?

Like a prostitute with aspirations, Boxiana has long since moved out from under the smoky lights of East Coast clubs to the garish ones of Las Vegas casinos. And here we are, still squinting in the cheap seats hoping to see something sublime.

Liebling preferred the cheap seats. Instead of sitting in press row, he was known to buy a ticket and squeeze his girth between fellow fans. He understood that the cast of characters at fight-time is not limited to the ring and that a good story is larger than its singular parts. As a result, he could be counted on to expand both the scope and the spirit of the simplest event into a kind of literature that cannot bore.

In 1956, The Viking Press published a collection of his work, and Liebling became an unlikely prince. *The Sweet Science* is the diamond he slipped on boxing's soiled finger. It was brilliant enough to be honored by Modern Library as one of the "100 Best Nonfiction" books of the twentieth century. In 2002, *Sports Illustrated* announced it as the greatest sports book ever written.

The Sweet Science begins with a whimsical exercise where Liebling establishes a credential that has nothing to do with his curriculum vitae. He relates being punched, "for pedagogical example," by a light heavyweight of the early twentieth century named Philadelphia Jack O'Brien. Readers are then reminded that O'Brien had fought Bob Fitzsimmons who had fought Gentleman Jim Corbett who had fought John L. Sullivan—and on down the line until a bridge of sorts was built between Liebling and the bare knuckles of Jem Mace.

Given his origins in the Upper East Side of Manhattan; given also his sedate lifestyle and beluga body shape, I suspect that the auspicious punch he received from O'Brien was no more hurtful than an idle breeze. In point of fact, by the time he socked Liebling,

O'Brien was the proprietor of a gymnasium on Broadway that catered to middle-aged men. Its letterhead proclaimed "Boxing Taught Without Punishment."

The sign outside the gym in the basement of the Boston YMCA on Huntington Avenue could have read "Abandon All Hope, Ye Who Enter Here." My escort to that threshold was black-eyed Boxiana herself. She found me on a street corner.

I was born and raised in a Boston housing complex where criminological variables congealed like one of Liebling's favorite French dishes. Although poor and fatherless, my disadvantages shrank when I was taught how to fight by an older teenage rebel who lived four courts away. To prepare for weekend rumbles or simply to stay warm in coatless winters, my friend and I would spar in parking lots, bare-knuckled like Jem Mace.

The son of a professional boxer out of Akron, Ohio, he was knocking out grown men while still a sophomore in high school and earned a reputation in the southwest neighborhoods of the city. The rumor mill said that he had something in his fists during those street fights, so he would routinely open his hands for bystanders when challenged. What followed would last only so long as it took him to land one shot. As sidekicks moved in to drag another cataleptic champion off the pavement, he'd open his hands again and laugh as he did.

His name was Rodney Toney.

By the late 1980s, Rodney had left West Roxbury High School and become a decorated amateur. He was recruited into junior middleweight champion Terry Norris's training camp in Campo, California, and turned professional. Those heavy hands of his earned him a moniker—*The Punisher*.

Meanwhile, I got civilized and turned up at Northeastern University on a Pell Grant. After classes three evenings a week, I'd box at the YMCA where the stink and the blood and the grunts re-established the distance between me and the middle class. I was, however, a two-timer destined to learn the hard way just how jealous a mistress Boxiana could be. Academia was her rival. She too had to be flattered. I'd skip roadwork to study and read a book between sparring sessions.

I got away with it for a while.

The gym was crowded on the day my two-timing ways caught up with me. The lamp Boxiana threw at my head was in the form of a left hook from the ninth-ranked middleweight of the world. That lamp of a left hook brought tears to my eyes. It still does, though for different reasons. You see, that punch was just as auspicious as the one Liebling took.

Its lineage began in the summer of 1925, when an extraordinary fighter named Harry Greb defended his middleweight title against Mickey Walker. He punched Walker on the nose and everywhere else and snapped his three-year, twenty-seven-fight winning streak. Seven years later, an aging Walker punched Max Schmeling as hard as he could but couldn't knock him down. In 1936, Schmeling punched Joe Louis as hard as he could and did knock him down. Louis landed a few solid ones on Ezzard Charles in September 1950, who landed many more on Joey Maxim eight months after that.

Maxim had a hard time finding Sugar Ray Robinson under a blazing sun in July 1952, but as Robinson began to suffer from heatstroke, Maxim zeroed in. Robinson's last bout was against Joey Archer in 1965. Archer's last bout was against Emile Griffith in 1967. Griffith's last bout was against Alan Minter in 1977. Three years went by, and a bloodied Minter watched his shots bounce off of Marvelous Marvin Hagler's chin like tin cans off a curbstone. Another three years went by and Hagler missed more than he landed on a rejuvenated Roberto Duran.

Duran was still in the third of what would be a five-decade career when he knocked journeyman Ricky Stackhouse down with a five-punch combination in the eighth round. By the time Stackhouse faced Charles "The Hatchet" Brewer in 1992, he was banned for health reasons from fighting in Florida and New York. Stackhouse was blasted out in three rounds. The fight was in New Jersey. His last fight was in Florida.

Brewer faced a healthier and far more dangerous middleweight at Foxwoods Casino in the fall of 1994. It was a thrilling brawl that took place seventy years after Greb and Walker's thrilling brawl at the Polo Grounds.

Brewer's opponent was Boston's own Rodney "The Punisher" Toney. All the bums from the neighborhood were there, including this one.

We sparred after that fight. I punched him hard, but he punched me harder and dented my nose. Blood flowed. Liebling showed me how much history flowed with it. There are fifteen degrees of separation and no less than ten International Boxing Hall of Famers connecting Greb's fist to my face.

When I think of it like that, even the post-nasal drip doesn't taste so bad.

SPRINGS TOLEDO
Boston, 2013

THE IMMORTALS

The Immortals:
Jewish Fighters Ancient and Modern

The Jew has made a marvelous fight in this world, in all the ages; and had done it with his hands tied behind him... All things are mortal but the Jew. All other forces pass, but he remains. What is the secret of his immortality? —Mark Twain

The First Jewish-Roman War began in the desert surrounding Jerusalem in 66 CE. It reached its climax in the Temple and ended at a place called Masada. A mercurial party called the Zealots provoked the war in response to Rome's affronts to their ancient beliefs. They didn't wave a flag; they waved Torah scrolls.

To Rome, the Jews' stubborn adherence to the idea of one god was odd. Other subject nations recognized a mishmash of gods, so the introduction of a deified human emperor was met with a shrug of shoulders—more incense was simply added to the cauldrons. The Jews were different. They'd jump in the cauldrons themselves before addressing a pagan emperor as "Lord." Those scrolls they waved left no room for compromise: "I am the Lord your God," thundered the first commandment, "you shall not have other gods before me."

Chronicles of the war bleed with examples of their religious devotion. The odds against them meant nothing. The horrors awaiting them in the Roman arena meant nothing. "There was no one," wrote a contemporary witness, "who was not amazed at their steadfastness and—call it what you will—the madness or the strength of mind of these victims."

The madness or the strength of mind.

When Titus sent his legions in to attack the Temple itself, he was aiming for the heart of the revolt. The entire population of Jerusalem rose up to defend it. Ordinary people fought in the forecourt while the rich fought in the inner courts. "The priests," a Roman historian recorded, "defended the Temple building itself" even as it burned. "With an undiminished excess of strength and courage, they tried to repel [the legionaries]" and, we are told, they "took no account of their own lives."

It was in vain. The Temple was defiled and destroyed and Jerusalem was left for the jackals. Remnants of the rebel fighters fled to where it all began—the desert.

Like a rose sprouting out of parched ground, Judaism began in the desert. Bound by a faith so radical it provoked wars with neighbors, the ancient Israelites could never bring themselves to forsake their faith. They could never bring themselves to forsake *him*. Their faith, after all, is not based on a set of ideas interchangeable with any others; it is based on friendship.

It began with the command of a singular god to a simple man. The man was a nomadic herdsman named Abram who called on the Almighty by name, who visited him and was visited by him. They engaged in conversations. Gifts were given. At times they'd argue. The fact that Abram's friend had made the world and was the source of all life was almost incidental; two persons reached out and made bonds of loyalty. God promised Abram that his children would survive every persecution and that they would be a holy people set apart from the rest.

They've been on the defensive ever since.

In 1920, the Walker Law legalized boxing in New York and tough urban Jews found a new home that was twenty feet square with ropes for walls and no roof to speak of. They trained at boxing's "Holy of Holies," Stillman's Gym on Eighth Avenue. The proprietor was a Jew. At Madison Square Garden, the first main event under the new law pitted Joe Welling against Johnny Dundee, and this time the Jew defeated the Roman.

By the end of the decade, Jews filled the ranks of fighters, managers, trainers, and cut men to become the dominant ethnic group in the sport.

Scattered though they were throughout the rest of the world, they were, spiritually speaking, bound together like the braids of a challah. In August 1929, sixty-seven Jews were killed and synagogues were ransacked in Hebron by an Arab mob. The boxing community staged a benefit at the Garden for the Palestine Emergency Fund. Congressmen, judges, U.S. Attorneys, and Tammany politicians took their seats amid more than sixteen thousand fellow fight fans. The five headliners were Maxie Rosenbloom, Al Singer, Kid Berg, Ruby Goldstein, and Yale Okun—all Jewish, all victorious.

It wasn't always so easy. Charley Phil Rosenberg fought during that era as well. "I was a bad boy when I was boxing," he told Peter Heller. "Every town I went to I started trouble in." Just a month after he won the world bantamweight title at the Garden, he was in Ohio facing an undefeated prospect. Someone at ringside kept shouting, "Kill the Jew bastard!" and Rosenberg finally had enough. He stood up from his stool, leaned over the ropes with a mouth full of blood and water and spit it right in his face. It was the mayor of Toledo.

Ray Arcel was Rosenberg's trainer. He was with the group of fighters that first walked into Stillman's Gym and anointed it. He later trained Barney Ross—an orthodox Jew born Barnet David Rasofsky who was the last of the great Jewish champions. In 1937, Ross was getting ready to defend his welterweight title against Ceferino Garcia, a Filipino puncher with more knockouts than Manny Pacquiao has bouts. Two days before the event, Ross fractured his right thumb. He refused his manager's pleadings to postpone the fight, so Arcel was sent in to talk to the champion:

"I says, 'Barney, why sacrifice?'"

"I don't sacrifice anything," replied Ross. "I don't need the right hand."

Ross hurt his left hand too in the second round and won anyway. The master-boxer did it with not much more than a left jab "—and," Arcel added with a finger on a temple, "a brain."

Sometimes even that wasn't enough. Ross, for all his ring savvy, couldn't handle Henry Armstrong. He had always said that he would take only one beating in his career, and in 1938, he took it. Arcel was among the corner men trying to stop his title defense against the relentless Armstrong after the seventh round, and then again after the twelfth. Ross refused to let them despite the pain and the blood.

Surrender was not an option.

Ross lost his title that night. As he descended the four steps at ringside with his right eye closed and his face a mass of cuts and welts, Grantland Rice called out from press row:

"Why didn't you quit? Did you want to get killed?"

"Champs privilege," was the reply.

As he walked down the aisle, Ross noticed something strange: "I don't hear any shouting. I don't even hear talking. I saw faces, faces, faces and they were all looking at me, not up at the ring." Thirty-five thousand fans in the Madison Square Garden Bowl watched him go in silence, in awe.

It was a tribute.

In 73 CE, the Jewish-Roman War came to an end. Masada, looming then as it does now in the Judean desert, had become a refugee camp for rebels fleeing Jerusalem. The Tenth Legion soon arrived. Hopelessly outnumbered men, women, and children—Zealots and their families—resisted for months a siege conducted by six thousand Romans. Ballistae hurled stones and fire at the great fortress day and night while engineers built a rampart. After they constructed a battering ram at the foot of the rampart, things got desperate. The walls started to shake amid soldiers' shouts and falling debris.

For those holed up inside, surrender was not an option.

On the eve of Passover, the Jews buried their sacred possessions and set their living quarters ablaze. The details are unclear, but it appears that they drew lots and quietly killed each other by consent. The next morning the Romans swarmed into Masada expecting fierce resistance. What they got instead was an unforgettable sight, a testament to the depth of the Jewish fist.

Nine hundred and sixty lay still, their blue and white prayer shawls flapping in the wind. Buried beneath the stones are parchment scrolls— prophecies, chronicles, and songs. "Have mercy on me, God, for I am treated harshly," reads one of them:

> Attackers press me all the day.
> ...O Most High, when I am afraid,
> in you I place my trust.
> God, I praise your promise;
> in you I trust, I do not fear.
> What can mere flesh do to me?

Crows circle over the desert scene while the Roman rank and file wander among the dead. They are not triumphant. They know that their enemy prostrated themselves to a power greater than Rome, a power that inspires acts and endurance beyond the scope of human comprehension. One by one, bronze helmets are removed. Battle-hardened soldiers stand in silence—in awe.

Time stops under a blazing sun,
and then begins again.

June 27, 2010

Fireworks and Falling Giants

Nothing so challenges the American spirit as tackling the biggest job on earth. —Lyndon B. Johnson

This Fourth of July marks the two hundred thirty-third anniversary of the Declaration of Independence. That document, affixed with the elegant signatures of unruly American colonists, provoked the giant that was Great Britain, and the world would never be the same again. The giant appeared eight days later as a fleet of warships sailing up the Verrazano Narrows in New York "like a forest of pine trees with their branches trimmed."

"We must all hang together," quipped Benjamin Franklin at the sight, "or assuredly we shall all hang separately." The patriots not only hung together, they implemented an unorthodox, and by some measures, absurd strategy to score a technical knockout.

The Fourth of July also marks the anniversary of Jack Dempsey's destruction of another giant—world heavyweight champion Jess Willard. There was nothing elegant about it. Dempsey had already made short work of Fred Fulton and Carl Morris, fighters that today could satisfy the definition of "super heavyweight," but Willard was something else. Known as the "Pottawatomie Giant," Willard was over six feet six inches tall and weighed two hundred forty-five pounds.

Gunboat Smith also fought Willard. He told Peter Heller that early on he threw a good shot at Willard and "his hair wiggled a little bit. That's all. I said 'Holy Jesus, that was my best punch, no detours, right from the floor, right on his chin.'" Smith decided to move around him and box him from a safe distance. In the tenth round, a frustrated Willard said, "Come on out here and fight, you big bum."

"Big bum?" Smith laughed. "[I was] hiding behind his god-damned leg!"

Like Smith, General George Washington spent the early part of his struggle against a superior force attacking and losing. Only after he began keeping his army on the move, essentially luring the Redcoats into the late rounds, did the tide turn. It was a revolution won by patience.

A patriotic American with Cherokee blood in him, Dempsey turned the theory of strategic retreat on its head. His fighting style was anything but patient. It called to mind a drowning man in a whirlpool. At six feet one and one hundred eighty pounds, he was even smaller than Gunboat Smith. He looked like a wee lad next to the champion, so they tacked seven pounds on his official weight to make it look better.

Willard's fight plan was similar to Great Britain's in that it was both conservative and overwhelming. He sought to line up the smaller opponent at the end of long jab and bomb him into submission. Dempsey fought out of a semi-crouch, and Willard planned to flick that hanging jaw to the moon. It was no secret that Willard had killed a man with a right uppercut in 1913. Some claimed it broke his neck.

The giant wasn't an active champion, however. He was even making a go in the entertainment industry. The *New York Times* carried ads in the sports section for *The Challenge of Chance*, which was playing in movie houses in the summer of 1919. In his role as a heroic ranch foreman, Willard swung his mighty arms, and upwards of twenty assailants tumbled down "like tenpins."

Dempsey's sparring partners included Big Bill Tate, who was of comparable size to Willard, and the middleweight Jamaica Kid. Dempsey knocked Tate cold on June 24 and was chasing Jamaica

Kid out of the ring. There was talk of his being "too fine," that he had peaked too early and had to be restrained from overtraining.

Forget the "Long Count Fight" eight years later against Gene Tunney. Dempsey had fear and death on his mind in Toledo. The mantra he'd mumble during a fight was brutally simple: "Kill him, kill him, kill him." By the time he lost to Tunney, he had long since brushed off the muck of the bordellos from whence he came and was extending his pinky in tea rooms with celebrities.

Forget the stories about Dempsey loading his glove with an iron bolt or using plaster of Paris against Willard. Both fighters inspected each other's wrapped hands in the ring before the gloves went on and the gloves went on under supervision. A contemporary described the force of Dempsey's punches as about equal to the "kick of an army mule in a tantrum." It's as simple as that. Over half of his wins up to that point came by knockout in one or two rounds, and the gloves used on that hot afternoon were only five ounces. Interestingly, the ring was not the regulation twenty-four square foot ring but only twenty square feet, to accommodate extra press rows. When Dempsey was informed of this change, he snapped, "You can make it fifteen square for all I care."

The fact is, he was afraid. Years later he told the *Toledo Blade*, "I took one look at Jess and said to myself, 'you're not fighting for the title, you're fighting for your life.'"

Dempsey came wild-eyed out of his corner at the first bell. The giant threw a one-two that did no damage, and then a jab that was slipped. They clinched and Dempsey can be seen on film with his open gloves on the crook of Willard's arms to guard against uppercuts. The referee separated them and Dempsey, itching to unload his artillery, galloped in behind a vicious right to the body, followed by a left hook to the head, a right, and a finishing left hook that sent Willard down for the first time in his career. Willard later said that he didn't recover from that left hook until about an hour after he left the ring.

There were six more knockdowns in round one and the star-spangled beat down continued for another two rounds until a bloody towel sailed into the ring and Dempsey became king.

America's birthday is on the horizon, but the prospect of an American heavyweight champion is not. Today, the dominant superpower of the ring is the same size as Jess Willard, with a similar fighting style and disposition. Ukrainian heavyweight Wladimir Klitschko has dominated freedom-loving Chris Byrd, Calvin Brock, Ray Austin, Lamon Brewster, Tony Thompson, and Hasim Rahman, stopping them all.

Only Brewster had success against Klitschko, and only in their first fight, where he was losing right up to the moment he landed a left hook, right cross, left hook combination that turned Klitschko's legs to lokshyna.

Since then, the giant's fights have been glorified sparring sessions. He is typically fought from the wrong range by second-rate guys who are content to allow him to play tyrant and dictate everything that goes on. American heavyweights, once hailed around the world for their ferocity, seem to be ailing from acute testosterone deficiency. They get an opportunity of a lifetime and then spend rounds passively looking for proof that they are outgunned by Klitschko. Boxing fans watch reruns of masochism evolving into surrender.

Whatever happened to the motto "don't tread on me?"

American heavyweights are indeed outgunned—no less than the citizen-soldiers at Breeds Hill or Saratoga. No less than Jack Dempsey. But neither those patriots nor the Manassa Mauler behaved as if their downfall was written in the heavens. No, they rewrote the script: shake your fist at the giant and blast away until you stand on his collapsed frame.

Klitschko may seem like an empire unto himself, but he is no more unbeatable than Willard was ninety years ago.

Despite what some commentators would have you believe, Klitschko is not a technician in the strict sense of the word. He uses a simple strategy that he follows to the letter, but has not progressed beyond that. He does a few things well, but where is the counter-punching skill, infighting, combination punching, body punching, or serious defensive technique? Klitschko has a jab that is sometimes pawing but that can also be of the Sonny Liston-lamppost type. He has a hard right and a devastating left hook. His defense consists of clinches and retreats. That's more or less the extent of his repertoire. It is certainly true that he hasn't had a compelling need to demonstrate other skills, but is that proof positive that his repertoire is any more extensive than we've seen? Unlikely. Boxers cannot hide what and who they are. It's his size that presents problems.

More important than the size of the car and what's under the hood is the psychology of who is driving. Klitschko has been stopped three times by aggressive men who bounced shots off his head until something inside him broke. When dealing with sustained aggression, he seems to panic. When hurt, he has been prone to come apart.

Brewster did several things in his first meeting with Klitschko that mirrored what Jack Dempsey did against Willard. He bobbed and weaved, slipped the jab, applied pressure, closed the distance quickly when Klitschko was in retreat, and punched in combination. Klitschko didn't punch himself out as claimed. His comfort zone was invaded by something irrational, and he was overwhelmed. His anxiety exhausted him. Unfortunately for the man known as "Relentless," the second time he fought Klitschko, he looked like he was standing in line at a bakery waiting for cherry pies—and he got dozens of them in the form of left jabs.

Giants tend to develop a fairly simple and laid-back style that is built around physical control of their opponent. "Once in a while," Willard admitted after the Dempsey fight, "I felt my head clearing and instinctively stuck out my long left which had served so well in previous fights. When I saw my opponent slipping easily past that protection, I realized that unless I landed a lucky blow, I was sure to lose."

Like the Willard jab, the Wlad jab is the primary instrument of oppression. A nervous jabbing contest may ensue that the smaller man can never win, and once he is lulled by the hypnotic tit-for-tat, the giant will suddenly commit to a right. Then it's tit-for-splat. Most of the hooks Klitschko throws are sweeping hooks that force his man to stay in front of him. When the opponent gets too close for comfort, he clinches and leans on him. It's all about control. He's hoping to wear the opponent out or convince him that it is futile to resist domination.

Trainers take note: Klitschko is not dangerous when his opponent is. He doesn't punch when he is being punched. This is not only a glimpse into an elemental weakness; it is a key to victory. Klitschko is cautious to a fault. He fights like a man carrying a priceless vase across a minefield, only the vase is his chin and the minefield has been a meadow.

The key is to take the control away from him by detonating explosives under his nose.

The key is to fight him like John Paul Jones would. With his ship sinking under the superior firepower of the British frigate *Serapis* and his crew decimated, the British captain asked Jones if he would surrender. Jones said: "I have not yet begun to fight!" One of his grenades flew into the main deck battery of the larger ship, ignited the casks of gunpowder, and the *Serapis* soon surrendered to the Americans.

Dempsey's grenades were no less deliberately launched than those of John Paul Jones. The film confirms that the only time he was at Willard's preferred range was when he was passing through to the inside—to the main deck battery if you will. He was either outside or inside of Willard's reach and never stayed where Willard could hit him and he couldn't hit Willard. To get close, he would get low and shoot in with slashing punches that forced the larger man on the defensive. Importantly, Dempsey punched with maximum leverage. He had disdain for anything less:

"I blasted him into helplessness by using my exploding fast-moving body-weight against him."

He blasted him into helplessness and upheld the great American tradition of beating the odds.

June 29, 2009

Kid Chocolate²

N *ew York.* He came with the heat in the summer of 1928. Wide-eyed and whippet-thin in the big city of dreams, he wore the only suit he owned. Six dollars and a one-way ticket stub from Cuba were in his pocket. His name was Eligio Sardiñas Montalvo.

He went straight to work fighting for chump change in smoky clubs in Mineola and Brooklyn. But he made gloomy faces light up, and word travelled about the eighteen-year-old boxer tearing up the locals. Soon the clubs were packed and ringside cynics were raising eyebrows. Damon Runyon called him a "stick o' licorice," others "the Cuban Bon-Bon," though his official *nom de guerre* was "Kid Chocolate." His style of fighting was something to behold; something new, something old. It brought a sweet whiff of nostalgia.

It was no coincidence.

Eligio was a barefoot newsboy in Havana when Jess Willard knocked out Jack Johnson and set off a boxing craze in Cuba that hasn't ended. It was said that he learned how to box by sneaking into bouts featuring Jack Britton, Johnny Dundee, and Young Wallace—all of whom fought in Havana during the 1920s. He'd sit mesmerized for hours in film houses as Joe Gans taught him how to jab and Jack Johnson taught him how to grab. His manager swore that his footwork was a mimic of no less than Benny Leonard.

"Boxing like a finished product of the old school," read the aptly-named *Painesville Telegraph* one morning in July 1929, "Kid Chocolate fought the nearest thing to a perfect fight. He hacked

21

away at his iron-jawed opponent with left jabs and right crosses, made a mug of him at long range," and flaunted the kind of timing and precision seen more in kitchens than in the swirling violence of prize rings.

In August, he thrashed a top contender at the Polo Grounds before fifty thousand, made a dollar for every seat filled, and became a sensation. Kid Chocolate was hot hot hot. In St. Louis, a teenage Henry Armstrong read a headline about the extravagant purse he earned for one night's work and said, "—That's for me." In Cincinnati, eleven-year-old Ezzard Charles heard about the taffy-colored suits with trick cuts, and when that gaudy touring car rolled into town, he said, "—That's for me."

But Kid Chocolate was more than the idol of black communities and the toast of New York City. He was the first Cuban world champion in history, an astonishing fighter who would take both the Jr. lightweight and featherweight crowns and face five Hall of Famers and eight world champions in a one-hundred forty-nine bout career. He was almost too big to fail. Almost.

On November 24, 1933, he fought Tony Canzoneri at Madison Square Garden. His prime ended that night, and Canzoneri seemed to find it amusing; he was grinning as he punched, like a man possessed. Edward J. Neil said the Kid gasped after taking a shot to those narrow ribs, and when another smashed into his jaw, his "long legs tangled all up as he floundered back into a neutral corner." Dazed, he fought back with the ferocity of a dying god and never saw the right hand that dropped him face-first to the canvas. He was counted out in the second round. Before the resin dust settled, the scribes said he was "headed for fistic oblivion."

They were wrong. He was already immortal.

On the undercard that Friday night, a teenage lightweight called *Cocoa Kid* fought a six-rounder. His manager sought flashy coattails and tried to pass him off as Cuban, though he was of Puerto Rican descent. Eleven years later, Cocoa Kid would mentor an African American swarmer at Stillman's Gym. The swarmer was billed as

"Chocolate Kid of Cuba" for his first three fights, though his right name was Calvin Coolidge Lytle (alias Bert Lytell) and he was from Texas. In San Diego, on the same day that Canzoneri knocked out Kid Chocolate, a bantamweight calling himself "Kid Chocolate" fought a four-rounder. Three nights later, another fighter calling himself "Kid Chocolate" fought an eight-rounder—in Malaysia.

It was only the beginning. Over seventy more namesakes in ten divisions carried the name into the 1960s and beyond.

New York, again. Although he didn't know it, middleweight Peter Quillin was following footsteps when he migrated to Manhattan in 2001. Eighteen and near-broke, the self-described *Cubano de corazón* from Grand Rapids, Michigan came for the same reason Eligio had seventy-three years earlier. He came seeking, he said, "changes for my life." It wasn't easy; no honest pursuit of glory can be. He worked at the International House of Pancakes, slept on a mattress found in the trash, and competed in New York Golden Gloves tournaments on an empty stomach.

But the heat was rising. In June 2005, Kid Chocolate came back.

Quillin, who had already adopted the moniker after trainers commented on his resemblance, turned professional. He went straight to work building a record only a stone's throw from where the immortal built his own record so long before. Quillin is familiar with the old fight films and those well-timed hooks and uppercuts made an obvious imprint. The "flashy confidence" did too: the 21st century's version of Kid Chocolate lights up opponents and then lights up gloomy faces with chocolate candies he tosses over the ropes after every victory.

Now fourth in the *Transnational Boxing Rankings*, Quillin is rising fast. He is 28-0 and is scheduled to fight in Brooklyn at the Barclay Arena on April 27. When the original Kid Chocolate was 28-0, he too was rising fast. And he fought in Brooklyn, just four miles east at the Broadway Arena on April 29.

I called Quillin recently and told him about the strange parallels, about how history seems to be repeating. He found it a little startling, as did I, before recognizing how inspiring the past can be when its hand is on your shoulder. When I told him that his predecessor scored a first-round knockout for his twenty-ninth win, he heated up. "I'm going for it! You'll see!" We will. We look forward to it.

Smoking isn't allowed in arenas anymore, but the ringside cynics remain. And we're still dazzled by Kid Chocolate's style of fighting. It's something to behold; something new, something old.

A sweet whiff of nostalgia.

A hand on a shoulder.

February 5, 2013

Alexis Arguello

Lenny Mancini sat in a wheelchair at ringside on the night of October 3, 1981. In the archives of the old man's head were images of a fight that never happened—his title shot against Sammy "The Clutch" Angott. Negotiations were in progress when Mancini was drafted into the army a month after the attack on Pearl Harbor. He requested a six week furlough and offered to donate the entire purse to the Army Relief Fund, but was turned down. Lenny was hit by mortar shrapnel in France and got a purple heart, but he never got that title shot. It left a hole in his life.

When he was forty-one years old, his third child was born; a son.

His son had fifty fights as an amateur, developed a swarming style reminiscent of his father's and was bequeathed his nickname: "Boom Boom." With a promise that he would complete the Mancini boxing legacy and become lightweight champion for both of them, Boom Boom went big time.

This was supposed to be the night of dreams. Twenty-year-old Ray Mancini stepped into the ring with a record of 20-0 with fifteen knockouts and the build of a brawler. Like Rocky Marciano and a host of others from boxing's golden era, he fought with the kind of ethnic, neighborhood, and familial pride perfected by Italian Americans. There's power in that hot blood. Like another left-hooker in Smokin' Joe Frazier, he was a converted southpaw, so his lead hand was souped-up. Ray's assets didn't stop there. His movie-star good looks suggested neither the heart of a lion, which he had, nor that he was a student of boxing history, which he was. The kid was a bello bull with brains.

The lightweight titlist standing across the ring was shaped like a whip. At almost five feet ten inches he was known as the "Explosive Thin Man," and with a record of 72-5 with fifty-seven knockouts, he was a veteran of many wars. In 1974, he knocked out his idol Ruben Olivares and became a featherweight titlist. He went to Ruben's dressing room after that bout and got down on his knees with a promise of his own: "I will defend this title with every drop of my blood." In 1981, he took a lightweight title from Scotland's Jim Watt. Afterward, he told the man he had just defeated that he would defend it for him with his blood and his heart.

And he did. He insisted on fighting the finest challengers and defended his belts twenty-two times in four divisions by the time he was finished. The Thin Man was also a technician extraordinaire. Snapshots of the hook off the jab that finished Alfredo Escalera in the thirteenth round of their rematch could be used in an instruction manual. It landed after a grueling trench war that left both victor and vanquished bloodied. His right hand was famous; it landed with an audible crack that set off car alarms outside casinos.

His name was Alexis Arguello.

The fight against Ray Mancini was Alexis's first defense of his third title. It was a classic. Lenny Mancini watched as his son mounted a relentless, two-fisted attack—the attack of two men. Incredibly, Ray was ahead after the twelfth round on two of the three judges' scorecards. But Alexis was a long-term investor. His mind was on the end, and he moved inexorably toward that end, eventually landing his money punch that sent Ray crashing to the canvas. Ray was tough enough to get up and fight on for another round, but his dream would be deferred. In the fourteenth round, Alexis landed a left hook, an uppercut, two more left hooks, and then a right cross. Ray went down again and the fight was stopped.

Lenny Mancini's eyes fell to the floor for a moment and then found Ray, who was being assisted back to his corner by the referee. Alexis's celebration was restrained. He saw the man in the wheelchair, leaned over the ropes and called out, "I'm sorry, I'm sorry."

Minutes later, Alexis was being interviewed in the ring. Ray walked over and Alexis's eyes lit up when he saw him. He clasped the challenger's hand and embraced him. "Good, good, good, good," Alexis strained to express himself in English but communicated his affection as flawlessly as any Italian. He pinched his cheek. "I love your father," he said. "That's the most beautiful thing you have." He offered encouragement: "I promise if I can do something for you, let me know, please, okay?" He said these things with the tip of his thumb touching his first fingers like an honorary paisan. Alexis knew about the elder Mancini's dream, about Sammy Angott, about the draft. On the way out of the ring, he took the old man's hand. "I'm sorry; it's my job," he said. "I love your son."

At the press conference, Alexis quietly spoke to Ray about how he himself lost his first title shot when he was barely past twenty himself, how he cried, and how he won it in his second try.

Ray too would win a title in his second try only seven months later. He did it in one round. His parents celebrated in the ring with him. Alexis was there.

Four months later, Alexis fought southpaw James "Bubba" Busceme in Busceme's hometown of Beaumont, Texas. Reporters noticed that after Alexis stopped him in the sixth round, he took Busceme's head in his gloves. "I told him that he was a man," Alexis said in the dressing room. "I wanted him to feel strong again, and give him his pride back. I told him he fought like a man, just like Mancini." The day after the bout, Bubba Busceme was in a local restaurant celebrating his thirtieth birthday. Alexis brought him a cake. Busceme, now fifty-seven, asked the *Beaumont Enterprise*, "How many guys would do that? How many world champion boxers would bring the person they just fought a cake?"

Roberto Elizondo, who was also knocked out by Arguello, told the *San Antonio Express-News* that Alexis "was always very gracious to me and my family. He was one of the best."

When Jim Watt was introduced at the weigh-in at Wembley before their bout, Alexis was in the background, clapping for him. "Be nice with everyone," Arguello told reporters in 1982. "That's the most important thing I've learned in fourteen years of fighting."

Aaron Pryor, who stopped Alexis twice, speaks now of how Alexis taught him to carry himself with dignity in public and how they became friends the moment they shed tears together after their rematch—Alexis in his disappointment and Aaron for Alexis. "I'm finished," Alexis said as he stood in defeat, head bowed.

The tears of Aaron Pryor mingle with millions now.

Alexis's body was found in his home with a hole in the heart on July 1, 2009. News reports said there were no signs of violence in the room and that traces of gunpowder were found on his hands.

Officials in Nicaragua confirmed that he shot himself in the chest with a 9mm pistol.

Gary Smith's *Sports Illustrated* profile of Arguello in 1985 tells the story of his father's attempt to commit suicide by jumping headlong into a well. He survived the fall, but when they lowered a chair tied to a rope, he took the rope off the chair and looped it around his neck, then yelled, "¡Hale!" (Pull!) Despite his efforts, he survived.

Alexis was six. By the time he was fourteen, he had found boxing.

The sweet science anchored him. It is a common irony among fighters that see the ring as a safe harbor. For him, it was a place of clarity, a place where his compassion followed his competitiveness on a valiant platform. "I am a reincarnated gladiator," he told Smith. Indeed. Gladiators faced their mortality in the arena but were exempt from the distressing uncertainty of civilian life. They lived to fight and fought to live, and there were no devils because there were no details. Their economy could be placed on a single coin—on one side was life/victory, on the other death/defeat. Combat is simple,

the objective clear. It is outside the arena where things get complicated. Ask Mike Tyson. "I thank God that I found something to
give me hope," Alexis said in an interview, "for giving me the chance
to be somebody."

After a fifteen-year career capped off by two legendary battles
with Pryor, Arguello retired. Depression set in. Addictions spiraled
out of control. The specter of suicide inherited, perhaps, from his
father began to whisper in his ear, pointing to the corruption of his
beloved country, the darkness in the world, the emptiness of his life.
The end was almost in 1984. Alexis, claimed Smith, sat in his yacht
off the coast of Florida with a gun to his head. Something dark whispered, "Hale." Pull. After several tense minutes and the pleadings of
his twelve-year-old son, he relented.

Alexis was staring into the abyss and the abyss was staring into
him. He returned to the ring briefly in 1985 and again in 1994. He
had to. It was safe there.

God knows he had issues. You don't watch your father try to kill
himself twice, grow up in poverty in a third world country, endure
war, exile, financial ruin, and the death of a younger brother—shot
and lit on fire as he lay on a pile of tires—and not have issues. For
Alexis, a living rebuke to the calloused brutes of pugilism's stereo-
type, these issues were magnified. Most of us natural cynics hear
about misery, corruption, or exploitation and shrug our shoulders.
This man would grow indignant or sink into a morass of despair.

He was interviewed by Peter Heller in 1986 and spoke openly
about how he was "lonely in the world," about how he did not want
to keep living because of the "wrong things" that seemed to be everywhere. Disturbingly, he wished that he could have "the guts" to
commit suicide: "I wish I could. I wish I could, Jesus Christ, leave
this place." Most retired boxers tell reporters that they want to find
a way to make a living. Alexis told them he wanted to find a way "to
live again."

Perhaps those dark whispers finally managed to drown out everything else. There can be little doubt that he was engaged in an inter-

nal back-and-forth battle that made his ring wars seem like Sunday strolls. Fifteen rounds? This looks like an existential crisis that lasted decades. Dr. Viktor E. Frankl, author of *Man's Search for Meaning* saw a powerful connection between feelings of meaninglessness and the neurotic triad of depression, aggression, and addiction. Suicide, he said, is depression's sequel.

Ray Mancini does not believe that Alexis Arguello committed suicide. "He was the face of Nicaragua," he told me recently. "He relished that. He loved that." However, there were allegations that his election last November as mayor of Managua was marred by ballot rigging and intimidation, and he himself was under investigation for misappropriating public funds. Perhaps he felt himself disgraced and, forgetting that he was a Roman Catholic, did what a Roman patrician might have done under the same circumstances—fell on his sword.

I don't know. I only wish that he had found a way to beat the count because those he left behind didn't hear a bell.

Thankfully, those he left behind still have his immortal image on fight films. We'll marvel at this legend all over again and affirm a spirit that surpassed even the level of his skill and the grandeur of his achievements. Despite his faults and failings, despite whatever happened at the end of his life, Alexis was noble. It should never be forgotten that during the last great era of boxing, he taught fatherless boys from poor neighborhoods all over the world about the divinity of kindness and the meaning of chivalry. I was among them. God knows we needed his example.

I hope he heard the applause of multitudes as he slipped between golden ropes to a place that's better than this, to a place where every tear is wiped away and broken hearts are healed.

Adios ...y gracias, Alexis Arguello, que brillan como el sol.

July 8, 2009

Black July

The quiet sun is mystifying astronomers all over the world. There has been no activity on its surface for months on end, no sunspots that would be expected to occur in a normal solar cycle. Some scientists believe that the sun is dimming.

This July is one of the coldest on record in many areas of the country. Here in stubborn New England, families are packing up the kids and heading to the beach the moment the temperature breaks sixty-eight degrees, in spite of the fact that it's ten degrees cooler on the shore. This is shaping up to be the Year Without a Summer, and we're all wondering what's going on.

Things are bad everywhere. Rising ranks of nouveau bums crowd out established bums for park bench real estate. The *Boston Globe*, which supplies blankets in sports pages, is facing bankruptcy after a hundred and thirty-seven years. It jumped up to a buck at the stand, and no one's buying what the Internet can supply for free. When you come across a newspaper wrapped around the leg of a park bench, be charitable and read it. Read how President Obama's approval rating is sinking back down to earth while the unemployment rate trudges up to 10%, the highest it's been in more than a quarter century. If you're feeling especially morbid, read about what seems to be an epidemic of suicide.

These are trying times.

It was a Jewish folktale that gave us the phrase "this too shall pass," and that means more than it seems when you think about it.

Everything is a matter of time. An active solar cycle will return and the temperatures will eventually normalize, the information industry will evolve, Obama's approval rating will climb and fall like every President's before him, and the economy will expand and contract. Hope will rise again. Time will see to it.

For flesh and blood, time begins as a courteous friend walking ahead and opening doors. It rewards our youthful energy with diplomas and promotions and titles. Then we age and stumble and can't keep up, and everything gets away from us. We shake a liver-spotted fist at the clock while clinging to times gone by like a drunk to a lamppost. The good ol' days we'll call them, and the older they are the better they'll be. Eventually, the friend from our youth will stop along the road. He'll turn and face us, and we'll gasp when we notice that he carries a sickle: Time, the destroyer.

The first moment of life begins the countdown to the last and our march toward it is written in the lines on our faces. It's all just a matter of time.

Is it really any wonder, then, that we seek out heroes, heroes that are at once timeless and transcendent?

Battling Blackjack (nee Lonnie Craft) was a heavyweight contender. In 1959, he killed his wife and was sentenced to be executed at Arizona State Prison. He walked to the gas chamber dressed as if he were walking to the ring, wearing boxing gloves, shoes, trunks, and robe. That may seem zany, but was it really? An ex-fighter needed to feel brave one more time, so he conjured up a heroic archetype and wore talismans.

There's a story from the 1930s about a condemned man in a North Carolina gas chamber. As potassium cyanide pellets were dropped in, a microphone caught his last words: *"Save me, Joe Louis; save me, Joe Louis; save me, Joe Louis."*

The boxer faces his mortality every time he steps through the ropes. He routinely asks the question that civilians can't bring themselves to ask until death is standing on the porch.

Stripped down to his trunks, stripped of all trivialities and pretenses, he is a man in dialogue with himself. That dialogue is as intimate as it gets, and the forum in which it happens is as public as it gets. The spectator in the stands witnesses the dialogue, and during a great fight, is spellbound by it. For him, comfort is derived from the vicarious experience of a great fight, precisely because the Grim Reaper is present in the ring. There, under the lights of an arena full of his eventual victims, the specter is taunted even as he points a bony finger. We love it.

Without really being conscious of it, we boxing fans are on sabbatical from a modern culture gone mad with political correctness. We lose ourselves in a celebration of ancient virtues, of masculinity. Need evidence? Watch the crowd as the bell rings to end a blazing round and you'll see graying men jump up and down like pogo sticks. Sometimes you'll see two strangers locked in an embrace, their heads craned toward the ring. Boxing can bring an almost spiritual exultation.

The gloved figure responsible for it has earned attention in the arts, literature, and politics. He has spawned countless references in slang and idioms that you hear every day from those who don't know the difference between Marciano and Graziano. He is and must be far more than a simple athlete. Athletes talk of sweat and tears but not blood. Strip away their size and ability to run and jump or hit a ball, ignore the bloated salary and celebrity, and something surprising might come into focus—their fields and courts are playgrounds.

The boxer is not even called an athlete. He is called a fighter, a gladiator, a conqueror, a king. He does not "play" boxing. Sometimes he fights as if his life is at stake. Sometimes it is. There are no helmets or shoulder pads for protection, and all vitals above the waist are laid bare. Like the laborer, soldier, scientist, craftsman, artist, and mechanic throughout human history, he will rely on his hands.

Great fighters have in some way conquered Time the Destroyer.

We carry them with us, in the cryogenic tanks of our hearts and collective memory, forever young, forever formidable, forever there to teach us courage in the face of ancient enemies like fear and death.

They are not supposed to die.

Alexis Arguello, Arturo Gatti, and Vernon Forrest went down for the long count on the first, eleventh, and twenty-fifth of July 2009. Alexis's death was ruled a suicide. Arturo's death was met with allegations that his fractious wife had killed him, only now it too is ruled a suicide. Vernon was shot multiple times in the back after he chased a robber with three guns, all of which were registered, two of which were his fists.

They were international representatives of the sweet science, and they represented it well. Vernon was a technician, Arturo a banger, Alexis, both. Ready smiles frozen in photographs reflect their immortal spirit as much as filmed chronicles of their wars.

They are not supposed to die. They are supposed to fade away; leaving heroes and myths intact as the rest of us march through this world as bravely as we can.

July 31, 2009

Force of Will

The strong men . . . coming on
The strong men gittin' stronger.
Strong men . . .
Stronger . . .
—Sterling Brown

J ames Kirkland sees no difference between boxing matches and turf wars. When that bell rings he isn't thinking about points, whether they be the finer points of technique or the ones those suits on stools keep track of. He isn't even thinking like a man; at times his bouts resemble primal clashes over hunting grounds and mating rights more than they do sports contests. Kirkland, an ex-convict, fights like someone who has suffered. The fact that much of his suffering was the direct result of his own bad decisions is beside the point.

Joseph William Frazier was born in 1944, the youngest of twelve children raised on a sharecropper's farm in Beaufort, South Carolina during the bad old days of Jim Crow. His kinfolk worked from sunup to sundown and at year's end had little more to show for it than did the slaves they were descended from. Most of them never left the region.

When he was twelve, "Billy Boy," as he was called, would go out to the mule shack and punch a burlap sack filled with sand and rags. It might as well have been filled with stardust. His chubby left arm began to crook and smash into the side of that sack with startling force. When he was fifteen, someone went and talked about his mother. Both chubby arms lashed out and got him suspended from school. He never went back. He got a job driving a tractor and hauling water, but had a run-in with the boss man and had to flee the region like so many other black men too strong to hold their hats in hand and too smart to stick around. He went north in 1959, just another nameless face among the millions in what historians call the Great Migration. He was a part-time car thief in New York City, and slept on a chair for two years in a crowded apartment.

Then Philadelphia beckoned.

Philadelphia—where fighters rise out of the cracked concrete like black Spartans with rap sheets. He took a job in a slaughterhouse and punched hanging carcasses during breaks. At seventeen he walked into a gym on the north side of the city with his dreams. That was fifty years ago. The man who would become Smokin' Joe Frazier never really left.

Men who have suffered sometimes get sentimental about it. They seek it out. Some mutter the maxim "Life is hell" too many times and start embracing it: "Hell is life." Kirkland, like many devil-may-care brawlers, never feels so alive as when he is exchanging blows. He uses boxing to turn his frown upside down.

On Saturday night, Kirkland was in the ring against Alfredo Angulo, a brawler like himself. He went right to him at the opening bell and slammed hooks into his flanks and up the middle. Thirty seconds later, he bulled him into a corner and threw a straight left, then slipped to his right to avoid the counter. Angulo timed his slip and threw his own right, and Kirkland went down. His dysfunction was looking up.

Angulo's expression told us nothing. He's a stoic whose mug wouldn't change by a twitch whether he was in a state of ecstasy or having his toenails torn off with pliers. His actions, on the other hand, told us that he's a gambler. The moment Kirkland got up and the referee waved the two fighters to resume battle, Angulo emptied himself in a winner-take-all effort. He threw over seventy punches before the end of the round and landed over half of them.

Kirkland absorbed all of them. How?

Whatever put that stardust into Frazier's burlap sack in South Carolina happened to sprinkle some on an ex-con from Texas Saturday night. And that's as good an explanation as you'll find anywhere.

Angulo's exertions were for nothing. He punched himself out just as Kirkland began coming on again. It was a left hook that sent Angulo spinning down Queer Street. When he collapsed at the end of that unforgettable first round, Angulo's seconds frantically gestured for him to stay down for eight seconds, but he would have none of that. He got up immediately and hoped no one noticed that he ever went down in the first place. For the next five rounds, Angulo was only semi-conscious. He fought on. His expression, soon distorted by punishment, still hadn't changed.

Kirkland seemed to be enjoying it all.

In 1969, the New York Times carried an article about Joe Frazier entitled "The Killer," and the Los Angeles Times ran a three-part series called "Man or Machine?" Tapping typewriters described the fighter's strange enthusiasm in the ring as "savage glee" and "blood joy." They saw Frazier grinning a bloody grin and eagerly nodding his head after landing a left hook hard enough to crack the ribs of dead cows in a Philly slaughterhouse. When moved off balance or knocked backwards, he'd clap his hands and then trot right back into close quarters like it was home sweet home.

At one minute and fifty-nine seconds of round six, Kirkland was feeling very much alive. His punches were landing with startling force, one after another. The strong man was getting stronger, even as the spotlight shifted back to Angulo.

After being battered for five rounds, Angulo's offense had become feeble and his defense stultified. Now his body was shuddering under the weight of violence and sagging for the first time in his professional career. All that was left was his will.

When they saw that Angulo would accept his terrible fate standing up, some in the crowd at the Centro de Cancun began to shriek.

The referee jumped in, stopped the fight, and probably saved his life.

In 1975, at the end of the twelfth round in the third epic struggle between Frazier and Muhammad Ali, Frazier's face had become a bulging mess. He told trainer Eddie Futch that he couldn't see from the crouch position and Futch instructed him to "pull back a step and stand up" so that he could see better. But Ali picked up on the change and adjusted accordingly. He knocked Frazier's mouthpiece out of his mouth, over the ropes, and six rows back. Frazier was vulnerable and almost blind.

"I fought on," Frazier said afterward. "There was nothing else to do."

"—And these are the kind of fighters who get hurt seriously," Eddie Futch recalled. "Those who won't go down, who will stay there and absorb the punishment when their body is just not capable of handling it anymore. And their mind tells them to stay up, and their body just can't handle it."

In the corner before the beginning of the fifteenth round, the trainer looked at his fighter and said, "Joe, I'm going to stop it." Frazier pleaded, "No, no, no!" Futch put his hand on his shoulder and said, "Sit down son . . . no one will ever forget what you did here today."

We never did.

We never will.

Joe Frazier died last night in Philadelphia. He was diagnosed with liver cancer in late September and spent his last days at home surrounded by family. No merciful referee or wise trainer interfered while he battled on his own terms, and something tells me he wouldn't have had it any other way.

Joe Frazier's spirit will never die.

We saw it in the ring Saturday night.

We'll see it again.

November 8, 2011

The Nonpareil, Trainer:
What's Old School Is New Again

B*rockton, Massachusetts.* A man and his son stand outside of what appears to be an abandoned factory on Petronelli Way. Yellowing classifieds roll by like tumbleweeds under a glaring sun. The son shifts on his feet and shoots three punches in quick succession. His chin is tucked in, elbows close to his ribs, right shoulder hunched up, a southpaw. His father's watchful gaze fixes there and then returns to the street.

Empty buildings loom. Broken windows saw Brockton as it once was, back when it was the shoe manufacturing capital of the world, back when Rocky Marciano plodded through Field Park dreaming of the day he'd walk into the factory on Dover Street and retire his father. By 1969, less than ten of those factories remained as the city dissipated and depressed. That was the year Marciano died in a plane crash and a single mother named Ida Mae Hagler fled race riots in Newark to find refuge in Brockton. In 1980, her eldest son began a fearsome reign as middleweight champion, and for the next seven years, he would walk through this door with a cap on his bald head and a gym bag slung over his shoulder.

Today, a new southpaw stands at the door.

Within minutes, Goody Petronelli, half the team that trained and managed Marvelous Marvin Hagler to the throne, parks his gray Dodge 4x4 and walks down the hill. Blue eyes twinkle as he greets the man with a handshake and pats the boy on the back. He's aging well. The only thing bent about him is his nose. "Nice to see you," he says, reaching into his pocket for keys. Goody holds the door open and gestures to the man and his son—a trainer and his charge.

Upstairs is the legendary Petronelli Brothers Gym.

Close the door behind you. A time machine is taking us to the future of the sweet science; a future where the ghost of a murderous body puncher named Tony Zale is conjured up, where Sugar Ray Robinson demonstrates the "candy-cane" shot to the kidney on old VHS tapes, and an elderly man in a convalescent home teaches how to counter it. We're going to a place where old-fashioned values and old-school ring tactics are dusted off, polished, and presented on a platter to a novice with skyward aspirations. At the center of it all is his father, a thirty-four-year-old boxing trainer with a name you won't forget: *The Nonpareil Hilario.*

The Past, Tomorrow

Turon Andrade is fourteen years old. He stands five feet seven inches and weighs a hundred and fifteen pounds. His eyes meet yours when he speaks, though his voice is quiet, as if he expects you to lean in and listen. His overall presentation convinces even adults that he should be respected. He has the flip-side down too; he's secure enough with himself to be respectful.

If you know what to look for, boxers like Turon can be identified by idiosyncrasies specific to them. He'll tilt his head, roll a shoulder, or flutter his hands for no apparent reason. These look like nervous twitches. They're not. He moves gracefully and with a hint of hazard—like a big cat in the bush, or Shaft.

Training begins with shadowboxing. "I tell him he is not to trash-talk. He is not to gloat," Hilario says. "That is not the way of a great fighter; it is the way of an insecure person." In a culture where the self-esteem movement has adolescents teetering on pedestals never earned, where gangsta rap mocks all things decent and sensible, Hilario upholds time-honored demands of self-respect. "Hip hop culture has been lying to our children for years," he'll assert. "There is no substance to it. Being a man doesn't mean disrespecting women. It doesn't mean demeaning others because of who or what they are. It doesn't mean celebrating those who poison our people with drugs and negativity."

The bell rings. Hilario steps into the ring with body armor for drills and then works the mitts with Turon for several rounds. When instructed to do six minutes on the heavy bag, there's no eye-rolling or teeth-sucking typical of his age group. He nods his head and walks to that station. Nothing sags about him, not even his trunks.

Boxing has a way of punching right through the flimsy shield of false ego to expose the truth about a man. Any flaws underneath are forced to the surface: deficiency of will, low pain tolerance, self-consciousness, fear. This young fighter has a rare advantage. His father's approach to boxing is comprehensive, which means that training doesn't end when Turon leaves the gym. It is constant. Hilario spends nearly all his free time with his son and daughter. Their days are structured. They run on a track at a nearby community college and play tennis and chess. They haunt Barnes & Noble and read for hours, exchanging quotes. Some evenings are spent watching old films like *Body and Soul* and *The Defiant Ones*, which are then discussed as a family.

When Turon came home from school complaining about teachers who he felt were singling him out, his father listened patiently and then offered an unorthodox parental response:

"What do you do when you are under fire in the ring?"

Turon thought about it a moment. "I slip and move."

"You should do the same thing in school."

Advice in the gym becomes discussions at home, transforming the boxing ring into something bigger and whittling life down to its essentials. Turon's lesson about staying composed during sparring will help him remain composed elsewhere, and chances are good that it will be absorbed into his identity. Such "spiritual discussions" are "equal to fifteen rounds of training," Hilario says. "They elevate him."

The Cappiello Brothers' Boxing and Fitness Gym is a two-minute walk from the Petronelli's. Turon is scheduled to spar four rounds against a young amateur with a six-pound weight advantage. They sparred the week before and Turon took a beating in the third round. "I wanted to say, 'Pop, that's it for the day,'" Turon admits, "but then I thought, 'there's no time for that,'" and he continued on. It didn't get easier. That evening, father and son sat down. "Nobody goes shopping for thoughts," Turon was told. "Thoughts just come. We make a decision. We try to make the right decision."

The rematch today is different.

Turon circles to the left of his opponent and is tentative with the jab. He lands a straight left to the body, a mirror-image of Tony Zale's straight right to the body, and a hook that recalls his father's signature shot. In the third, a left hook echoes off his headgear like a gong. He holds on. The bell rings. In the corner, Hilario knows when to give instruction and when to give a boost and a boost is in order here. Turon does well in the fourth round with a masterful display of tilt jabs (i.e., jabbing with your opponent), body punching, and what Archie Moore called "escapology"—building a bridge even while attacking to escape quickly.

In this little comeback lie the seeds of far greater ones. Henry Wadsworth Longfellow muses unseen in a folding chair, ringside: *"In ourselves, our triumph and defeat."*

Turon is thinking not of the poet but of a pragmatist as he unwraps his hands. "Pop told me to 'Joe Frazier' him." When pressed for a definition of what a "Joe Frazier" is, he says, "I come in low, hands up, bobbing and weaving and 'sneaky' bump him—so it won't look like pushing—to get him moving back so I can counter and punch him while I'm moving forward."

"Pop teaches me a lot of angles, how to come in, how to spin out, stay balanced, and punch from both sides," Turon says. Already this budding stylist has better technique than half the professionals I've seen on cable.

Danye Thomas is a trainer at the Cappiello Brothers' gym. "The Nonpareil," he says, "is wise."

Time Passages

Hilario wasn't always wise. He was expelled from Brockton High School for fighting. He had just found boxing and had not yet internalized its demands for self-control, but he'd suggest that it wasn't an expulsion so much as a transfer. The Petronelli Gym became his new classroom, and Steve "The Celtic Warrior" Collins and Robbie Sims his tutors.

Sims took him under his wing, and before you could say "mahvelous," he won the silver mittens in his first amateur fight and then had sixty more, winning all but six. He sparred regularly with a professional named Ray Oliveira, a fixture on ESPN in the 1990s, and held his own. During the day he was in the gym or in the public library studying boxing history. At night he would pop fight films in a VCR and practice in the mirror for long hours.

He was sixteen years old when he met an antediluvian named John Bonner.

Bonner had two cousins who fought in the early twentieth century: Jimmy Bonner and Jack Bonner. The latter fought Jack Blackburn, a dangerous lightweight of the time who went on to train Joe Louis. The man who would become Hilario's mentor began life as an orphan. Raised in North Philadelphia, he spent his early years boxing in those tough gyms. In the 1940s he moved to New York City, where he would hang around Stillman's Gym and soak up an endless array of tricks from great champions training there. When he met Hilario, he was immediately impressed with the tendency of the young Kriolu to rattle off long-dead names—names Bonner himself hadn't heard in decades. The old man had found a worthy student and so bequeathed him all those tricks that no one knows anymore.

With aspirations of turning professional, Hilario followed in Bonner's footsteps to New York City. Indigent, he stayed in the Covenant House in Times Square though the connections he made were priceless. Stillman's Gym was shuttered in 1959, but he found Mark Breland at the New Bed-Stuy Boxing Center and the late Jose Torres in Michael Olajide's Kingsway Gym. Torres invited him to his home where Hilario stood, jaw-to-floor, in what was essentially a shrine to boxing and then to USA's *Tuesday Night Fights*, where Torres was the Spanish commentator.

On Fridays, Hilario took the train over to New Jersey to work with Al Certo and James "Buddy" McGirt, who was still swapping leather back then. "I felt like King Tut," he recalled. "Jose Torres on weekdays, Al Certo on weekends." Hilario jumped another train back to Brockton just in time to welcome his first-born son into the world (Turon), and then returned to Jersey.

Certo was as old school as they get. For him, training for a fight was all sparring and heavy bags. Speed bag platforms were empty. "—Fighters don't punch like that," he'd snap.

One day Hilario was in the ring and Certo stopped the session: "Hey Junior, what's on your mind baby?" It was his new family. Homesick, Hilario returned to Brockton. He turned up at the South Shore Gym in Whitman with a plan to turn professional close to home. His first fight was already scheduled when he asked a manager whom he'd be fighting. The response was a short right that he didn't see coming: "Never mind that, you're getting paid to fight." Time stood still for a moment, and then Hilario dropped the skip-rope and walked out. Like Bonner, he became a gym rat, honing his skills and trying not to think about depleting nickels.

An epiphany in the form of a parable changed everything:
A man was looking through a window for a teacher, but it was always blurry. For years he continued on his journey but would inevitably return to the window. One day, it became clear. He saw that it wasn't a window at all. It was a mirror. He himself was the teacher he was looking for.

The Nonpareil Hilario became a teacher. He has not discriminated in welcoming new disciples, extending his glove toward demographics once scorned in cauliflower alley, the beautiful people, white-collar professionals at the Beacon Hill Athletic Club, and suburban athletes who never trained in a gym that wasn't climate-controlled. But he wouldn't stray far from the more raw-boned venues he was familiar with. He trained several fighters in the Brockton area and worked in Buddy McGirt's gym in Florida with professionals Dat Nguyen, William Guthrie, and Jimmy Lange.

Two years ago, Turon asked his father to teach him the secrets of the sweet science.

The Future, Yesterday

John Bonner, the man who Hilario affectionately calls "Ray Arcel," now lives in a convalescent home in New Hampshire. He is eighty-eight years old. Hilario often brings his son to visit and they never leave empty-handed.

During one visit, Bonner described a move he picked up in North Philadelphia, a move that became Ray Robinson's candy-cane shot. Robinson would feint a jab and throw a right hook to the kidney. His glove would turn around mid-flight so that the back of his knuckles would land. Bonner described this and how to counter it: he said to "sit down" (i.e., assume a compact stance), twist with the shot as it whistles in to catch it on your elbow, and shoot an uppercut from the same side.

Bonner stands up to demonstrate such things from the gold mine of his memory and then collapses in his chair, exhausted, at the finish. Some of these moves haven't been seen in a boxing ring in over half a century. They are little resurrections. Turon watches intensely and then repeats the shot and the counter. His execution is perfect. The old man laughs and claps his hands.

The Nonpareil, with an eye on the past and the future, smiles knowingly.

August 17, 2009

THE LISTON CHRONICLES

Rising Sonny

An' the dawn comes up like thunder...
—Rudyard Kipling

Dick the Bruiser was built like the Hoover Dam. A former lineman for the Green Bay Packers, professional wrestler, and an icon from the 1950s through the 1980s, he stood six feet one and weighed two hundred and sixty-five pounds. When he spoke his mind, people listened. In 1962, he spoke his mind about what he saw as the sorry state of the heavyweight division. Charles "Sonny" Liston was the heavyweight champion at the time. Legend has it that Sonny got wind of what the Bruiser said and caught up with him out front of the Thunderbird Hotel in Las Vegas. Sonny beat him into a corner and slapped him repeatedly until he cowered on the sidewalk. Heralded as "The Most Dangerous Man Alive," Dick the Bruiser was overheard whimpering, "I just wanna go home now."

Legends spring up like black daisies on the road where history's tough guys swagger. Be they Goliath, Richard *Coeur de Lion*, or Frederick Barbarossa, reliable truths about their exploits have long since been stretched and snapped. And yet, despite expectations, most of the black daisies at Sonny Liston's feet are credible. They took root by the time he was a thirteen-year-old first grader (and that's not a misprint). He was functionally illiterate and had a juvenile record as long as his wingspan. He was a union strikebreaker for wise guys and served time in prison for armed robbery and assaulting a police officer.

That last conviction raised eyebrows. The cop in question pulled his gun on Sonny, but Sonny snatched it away and then did worse. Witnesses heard a voice saying, "don't hurt me" from the alley where Sonny had carried him. After splitting his eye seven stitches worth and breaking his knee, Sonny walked out of the darkness wearing the cop's hat and carrying his gun.

That cost him seven months in an eight-by-nine. But no sooner was he released than he got pinched again. This time it was for resisting arrest. Sonny had deposited another cop upside down in a trashcan.

In *The Devil and Sonny Liston*, by Nick Tosches, Captain John Doherty told about Sonny's struggles with the St. Louis Police Department—and the St. Louis Police Department's struggles with Sonny: "Five coppers tried to lock Sonny. This ain't no bullshit story. They broke hickory nightsticks over his head. They couldn't get his hands cuffed. He was a monster."

He was banned from fighting in several states, including New York and California, and if a man is to be judged by the company he keeps, they weren't wrong. There is little doubt that Sonny was connected to, if not outright "owned" by underworld figures operating out of St. Louis. However, the trajectory of his career does not suggest that he was given a steady diet of soft touches. Those behind him had confidence; only two of his first forty opponents had losing records. In his sixth fight, Sonny faced Johnny Summerlin, who was 19-1 and would crack the top ten within the year. Sonny beat him twice in a row.

In 1954, he fought an unorthodox light heavyweight named Marty Marshall. Marshall had a style that recalled the pivoting, herky-jerky, watch-me-ruin-your-timing style of Jersey Joe Walcott. He could switch from an orthodox to a southpaw stance on a dime. Sonny, who fought like a night train ever-rolling into KO station, had trouble with something that refused to stay on the tracks. He claimed that Marshall ran around the ring whooping like such a clown that he couldn't help but laugh—and got his jaw broken by a freak shot. In the sixth round, another shot fractured it again. Sonny dropped a split decision. "I walked the streets all night," he remembered, "it hurt so bad." The loss was twice avenged.

The third time Sonny and Marshall met was in March 1956. Marshall entered the ring as a replacement for Hall of Famer Harold Johnson, a supreme technician who had to back out of the bout after injuring his shoulder in training. At that juncture, Johnson's 55-8 record sparkled with wins over Jimmy Bivins, Bert Lytell, Archie Moore, Clarence Henry, and Ezzard Charles. It is very unusual to see a prospect with fourteen fights put at such risk so early.

In May 1956, Sonny broke the aforementioned cop's knee in the alley and ended up cooling his heels in the clink for months. He didn't return to the ring until 1958. By November, ringside observers said that he barely broke a sweat in eight victories.

In 1959, he entered his rampaging peak.

Sonny fought a heavy puncher named Mike DeJohn in 1959 when DeJohn was ranked eighth by THE RING. According to the *New York Times*, Sonny's jab made a mess of his nose, and De-John went down twice from body shots in a six-round slugfest. Two months later, Sonny faced the widely avoided Cleveland "Big Cat" Williams—another banger. Sonny stopped him in three rounds. He stopped him again a year later and a round sooner. (Williams, incidentally, wouldn't be stopped again until he met Muhammad Ali in 1966. By then Williams was shot, figuratively and literally.)

By the end of 1960, Sonny demolished Nino Valdes, bounced number-two contender Roy Harris off the canvas before stopping him in the first round, and then dropped number one contender Zora Folley twice on his face, the second time for keeps. Master boxer Eddie Machen, ranked third, went the distance. Sonny swung and missed and didn't look so formidable but took a decision anyway despite a three-point deduction for low blows.

Five of these six men were in their prime.

According to THE RING, Sonny was the number-one contender since at least July 1960 when he beat Zora Folley. Nat Fleischer, the magazine's highly respected editor, began demanding that Sonny be given a shot at Floyd Patterson's title as early as possible. Cus D'Amato, Patterson's manager, was in no rush to sign Valdes, Folley, or Machen, but the complicated shadow of Sonny Liston gave him real shivers. D'Amato avoided them all with loose and limber reasoning: he complained about the cheap prospective gate in a Machen fight, yet became a moralist when it came to Sonny and his shadowy management.

Sonny did two things of note during this time. The first is that he stayed active, even to the point of accepting the short money to fight Harris, Williams, and Zora Folley. (He took $25,000 to Folley's $40,000, despite the fact that Sonny was on another knockout streak and hadn't lost in seven years. Zora lost a fight less than two years before and had just won a snoozer against an opponent who had twice as many losses as wins.)

The second is that he decided that the obstacle on his road to the title was the manager of the man who held that title. With evil thoughts swirling in his mind, he took a train to New York and appeared in D'Amato's office unannounced. He got right to the point: "Is you or is you ain't going to give me a title shot?" Cus presumably came out from under the desk and told Sonny to give him a list of managers and Cus would choose one for Sonny himself. Sonny, who was smarter than the average bear, said, "Ain't that nice. What you mean is that you want to control me."

By the time Sonny fought Albert Westphal in December of 1961, he was fed up.

At the weigh-in on the day of the fight, Westphal was feeling the glare of the brooding behemoth. "You can talk to me. I'm your friend. Why are you so angry?" Westphal asked him. "You'll find out tonight," snapped Sonny. The German looked like an erratic kernel of popcorn until the roof fell in on him. The fight was over in two minutes.

By then, the popular Floyd Patterson was wrestling with his conscience: "One night in bed, I made up my mind. I knew if I wanted to sleep comfortably, I'd have to take on Liston." So, Patterson defied D'Amato's safety-first policy of title reigns, waved away the fears of the NAACP, and overruled the pleadings of no less than President John F. Kennedy himself. A quivering hand signed to fight Sonny, and Patterson bravely met his fate.

There was a collective gasp when Sonny became heavyweight champion of the whole damn world on September 25, 1962, at Chicago's Comiskey Park. "It was," wrote Arthur Daley, "a bull elephant matched against a frail deer and then felling him with a disdainful swipe of his ponderous trunk."

The "bad guy" won, just like Sonny had promised. The armed robber, labor goon, cop-fighting ex-convict was king. Jim Murray wrote that the world of sports had to reconcile itself with the fact that it was stuck with Sonny; indefinitely. It was as good as "finding a live bat on a string under your Christmas tree."

Somewhere amid the post-fight chaos, a twenty-year-old aspirant named Cassius Marcellus Clay hastily dashed down some verse:

> *"And as the people left the park*
> *You could hear them say*
> *Liston will stay king*
> *Until he meets that Clay..."*

May 28, 2009

Setting Sonny

Though the fury's hot and hard
I still see that cold graveyard
There's a solitary stone that's got your name on.
—Elvis Costello, 'Complicated Shadows'

LISTON was spelled out on the back of the heavyweight champion's robe when he walked into the weigh-in before his second title defense. Behind the lettering was the image of a sun—a setting sun.

Sonny Liston had every reason to be confident on the night of February 25, 1964. He was an eight-to-one favorite to defeat Cassius Clay. "The loud mouth from Louisville," declared the *New York Times*, "is likely to have a lot of vainglorious boasts jammed down his throat by a ham-like fist." That was an echo of the opinion of nearly everyone paying attention. Even the Nation of Islam was reluctant to get too involved on behalf of their recent convert. Elijah Muhammad himself believed it impossible for Clay to beat Liston. Malcolm X did not, and offered religious-based counsel to the jittery challenger, and then defied Elijah Muhammad by attending the fight in Miami.

Sonny didn't know it yet, but he had already made the mistake common to history's strong men. The mistake was hubris. His contempt for Clay was as pronounced as his training was casual. He drank wine and snacked on potato chips. He was prepared only to go the two or three rounds he figured it would take to cash in on Cassius; no more, no less.

The Liston training camp revolved around the whims and moods of Liston. Everyone, including his trainer Willie Reddish, was told what to do and when to do it. With James Brown's "Night Train" playing over and over on the phonograph, Sonny would go into a trance and keep time on the speed bag. He listened to no one except a Roman Catholic priest who befriended him and the only hero he ever acknowledged—Joe Louis. Apparently, Louis never told Sonny the story of his own lackadaisical training that brought about his first loss against Max Schmeling. Nor did the priest open the book of Samuel in Sonny's presence. Had he done so, the champion may have remembered that it was a mere stone in the sling of a youth that felled Goliath. No less was the speed of an arrow in the bow of a youth that slew Richard *Coeur de Lion*.

Sonny looked at Clay and saw a mere stone in his shoe and expected to parry his arrows as if they were shot by Cupid.

And so it went that a twenty-two-year-old upstart fought like an archer on wheels, and Sonny's clay feet followed as the rounds sailed past the third. The new old king learned the hard way that hubris blinds a man more than the astringent his corner may or may not have put on his gloves before the fourth round. Sonny refused to come out for the seventh round, and that was that. Cassius Clay became the new champ, shocking the world and bouncing all over the ring proclaiming exactly that while Sonny sagged on his stool.

Barbarossa, one of history's great warriors, fell off his horse and drowned under the weight of his armor in a shallow river. Sonny's fall was just as anticlimactic. It was downright meek.

Disrobed of his invincibility, he went to St. Francis Hospital for X-rays on his left shoulder. Later a team of doctors confirmed that he had in fact suffered an injury that would be "sufficient to incapacitate him and prevent him from defending himself." Sonny's corner claimed that the injury occurred during training and that they had to cease sparring earlier than planned. "We thought we could get away with it," they added.

A rematch was set for November 16, 1964, at Boston Garden.

Sonny trained harder than he had since his rampaging peak in 1959 on the grounds of what is now the White Cliffs Country Club in Plymouth, Massachusetts, whipping himself into search-and-destroy shape at two hundred and eight pounds. "Night Train" was shelved because the beat was too slow for a new pace of training. Reporters swarmed, and Sonny's mood swings were even worse than usual. Ten sparring partners became casualties. Some ended up in the hospital. Sonny was sending a message to the loudmouth who whipped him. "When I catch him," Sonny promised, "you'll know I'm bitter."

It wasn't all meanness with Sonny. He was known to be gentle with children and impulsively generous with the down-and-out. At times, he seemed to yearn for the kind of peace his life choices would never allow. One evening at White Cliffs, he noticed a scarlet sunset cascading across Cape Cod Bay. "Look at there," he said to a reporter for *Sports Illustrated*, extending his giant hand. "Isn't that the most beautifulest sight you've ever seen?"

He didn't know it yet, but that setting sun was inauspicious.

On Friday the 13th, Clay, who by then was calling himself Muhammad Ali, was rushed by ambulance to Boston City Hospital for an emergency hernia operation. The fight was called off. Sonny growled, "If he didn't carry on in the street the way he did he wouldn't have hurt himself." Ali was no less disappointed. "I was really in the best shape of my life as was Sonny. Now all that hard work has gone down the drain," he said. "Everything was set up. Now I have to sit back for another six months. It was such a letdown for me and for Sonny. All that work for a man his age."

A man his age. Liston dissipated. He was picked up for drunk driving in December and got into it with ten policemen who had to wrestle him into a cell. Reporters noticed that he was looking "heavier and haggard."

He spent Christmas in jail.

The infamous rematch ended up in a high school hockey arena in Lewiston, Maine. Ali came in four pounds lighter but was noticeably bigger than the previous year with inches added to his thighs, biceps, and forearms. Sonny was simply older. Whatever fire he had captured at White Cliffs was gone.

Suspiciously, Sonny was installed as a nine-to-five favorite.

Ali began round one bouncing and shifting and flicking shots. He landed one hard right hand, and Sonny reacted as if it were a caress. He was moving in when he threw a lazy left jab, and Ali, whose back was near the ropes, came over with a right hand that was far more innocent than the previous one . . . and Sonny went down. The fiasco that followed is incidental. Sonny's performance was anything but.

Some believe that Sonny's first round knockout was genuine. Others meet it halfway and consider the knockdown genuine but not his refusal to get up. Sonny himself spoke of it before the California Boxing Commission and stated that the knockdown was indeed real, but he refused to get up because Ali was standing over him. This doesn't fit the film. Sonny was too busy trying to make it look like he was hurt. He wasn't even looking at the big butterfly fluttering about.

Overlooked is Sonny's exceptional chin. Mike DeJohn proved it. Cleveland Williams proved it. Cops did too with their hickory nightsticks. After Marty Marshall landed the right that broke his jaw, he said, "I never knew he was hurt. You hit him with your Sunday punch but he don't grunt, groan, flinch or blink. He don't do nothing; he just keeps coming on. He's discouraging that way."

Ali landed a flicking punch thrown with his legs out of position and no leverage. His first response to Sonny's going down was outrage, and it is memorialized in perhaps the most famous boxing photograph ever snapped. "Get up you yellow dog!"—Ali's shout at the horizontal challenger is frozen in time. It was only later that Ali and company came up with the "anchor punch" spin for posterity's sake. It's understandable. A dive taints both fighters; a first round knockout of the impossibly strong Sonny Liston, by contrast, would be a fitting aftershock for the world.

For all Floyd Patterson knew, everything was on the level. He went to Sonny's dressing room after the bout. Sonny sat there alone, staring at something far off with that permanent scowl that wasn't a scowl. Floyd said, "I know how you feel. I've experienced this myself." Sonny didn't acknowledge him. Floyd turned and began walking out when Sonny came up behind him, put a hand on his shoulder and said, "Thanks."

Sonny became a pariah after that fight. He fought on against nondescript opposition in Sweden and then returned to fight a six feet four inch truck driver named Bill McMurray. Some believed that Sonny was forty years old by this point though he still had the strength of ten men.

With Ali stripped of his title and out of the picture, Sonny was fixing his sites on Joe Frazier by 1968. Emboldened by a fourth round knockout of McMurray, a new trainer in Dick Sadler (who would also train George Foreman), and Sammy Davis Jr. showing interest in his career, he was feeling upbeat. "I'll beat [Frazier]," he declared. "I won't have to chase him. It'll be like shooting fish in a barrel."

Henry Clark was ranked ninth by THE RING when Sonny faced him four months after McMurray. Liston won every round behind a jab and became the first man to stop him. Amos Lincoln was his eleventh straight knockout victim since the Ali rematch. He was draped over the ropes for three minutes while his handlers revived him.

The ex-champion was coming on strong, straight for Frazier, and the boxing world was buzzing. But it wouldn't last. If the word on the street was accurate, it couldn't last. The word said that Sonny was boozing it up regularly and addicted to heroin.

Leotis Martin brought the sheep in with a right hand, followed by a left hook and another right. Sonny fell hard and didn't move. No one doubted that the knockout was legit.

His last bout was held in Jersey City in June 1970 against Chuck Wepner. A strangely silent guest appeared at the back of the armory where the fight was held. It was Muhammad Ali. Ali remained confused and fascinated by Sonny for many years after their bouts, and admitted that the man scared him. He once went so far as to privately claim that "Liston was the Devil." Either way, Sonny was applauded as he entered the ring against the six feet five inch, two hundred and twenty-eight pound challenger.

It was a brutal fight, and Sonny won those.

Wepner was stopped after nine rounds. He was in shock for three days after the bout with a broken nose, a broken left cheekbone, and seventy-two stitches to close his face. Sonny had hopes that this, his fiftieth victory, would qualify him for more lucrative bouts. It was not to be.

The Grim Reaper showed up instead, tapping him on one of those massive shoulders. Sonny Liston died alone, probably on December 29, 1970, and apparently from a drug overdose. No one really knows. Black daisies sprang up in the bedroom where his body lay. It was days before anyone found him.

It had been a brutal life, and no one wins those.

June 1, 2009

The Conquering Sonny

Artillery is the god of war.
—Stalin

The grave of Sonny Liston is located just south of the children's section at Paradise Memorial Gardens in Las Vegas. His bones lie unsettled beneath the roar of airplanes and avenue traffic. Few visit. His image, sprawled out at the feet of an icon, can be found tacked up on bedroom walls of teenagers. To the uninitiated, the man on the canvas is just a nameless opponent of Muhammad Ali. To casual boxing fans, he is the "Big Ugly Bear" taking a dive. To many purists the image is an insult because they know that the Liston of 1959-1960 was among the most fearsome wrecking machines the heavyweight division has ever known.

It is time that we visit his grave, reanimate those unsettled bones, and give Sonny his due.

Boxing aficionados spend hours online, on street corners, and in bars and gyms debating hypothetical head-to-heads between fighters from different eras. The big boys of the heavyweight division can be counted on to detonate the biggest debates. Could Mike Tyson have overcome George Foreman? How about Rocky Marciano vs. Joe Frazier? Would Lennox Lewis have been too much for Jack Dempsey?

It is widely assumed that the greatest heavyweight who ever lived is either Ali or Joe Louis. The high level of Ali's competition and his penchant for winning critical bouts, even after the powers of youth had dwindled away, are two of the strongest arguments in his favor. Louis's twelve-year reign as champion is also a tough achievement to beat. "Greatness" is largely a question of resume. Who would have won had they faced each other is another question.

Max Schmeling beat Louis who beat Max Baer who beat Schmeling. Frazier beat Ali who beat Foreman who beat Frazier. Kenny Norton beat Ali who beat Foreman who beat Norton. Ring logic does not confirm that if A beats B, and B beats C, then A will beat C. That logic is disrupted by the old principle that "styles make fights" and there are a hundred examples.

This allows us to elaborate on an interesting question.

Consider the twenty-seven heavyweight kings of the modern era from Jack Dempsey to Wlad Klitschko. If each of them faced all of their peers in the respective primes of their careers, who would emerge with the best record?

Who would be the king of the hill?

At first glance, Liston looks like an unlikely contender in such a competition. His championship reign lasted through all of one defense. Sure, he had the misfortune of crossing paths with perhaps the greatest sports phenomenon of the twentieth century, but he was foolish enough to take him lightly. Then he squandered (or was forced to squander) his chance for redemption in the rematch. This isn't the stuff of a great championship reign, and I submit that any boxing writer who lists Sonny's reign anywhere near the top should be sent packing to Wimbledon where he can watch those other guys in shorts.

Many, however, suffer from Ali-induced myopia. They see Liston sagging on his stool in Miami or splayed on the canvas in Neil Leifer's iconic photograph and go no further. They forget that Liston began his disappointing title reign late due to his incarceration and Cus D'Amato's unwillingness to see Floyd Patterson face a real challenge. This much is certain: the fighter who stepped into the ring against Cassius Clay was not the fighter who stepped into the ring against Cleveland Williams five years earlier. That Liston, the

1959 pre-championship version, demands a closer look. He's the
sleeper in our king of the hill competition.

Physicality

Size isn't everything. Dempsey treated Jess Willard like a Kansas
tornado would a cull tree. Louis easily chopped down giants like
Primo Carnera, Abe Simon, and Buddy Baer. Size isn't everything,
but that's not to say it doesn't matter. A new breed of giants has
taken over the heavyweight division. Dempsey and Louis, at one
hundred eighty pounds and two hundred one pounds respectively,
may not have had enough physical strength to hold off the less lum-
bering giants of today, though they would have had the skill. Liston
had both.

With a wingspan as long as Lennox Lewis's at eighty-four inches, a fist that was by some reports fifteen inches around and there-
fore bigger than Willard's, Carnera's, both Klitschko brothers', and
Nicolay Valuev's, Liston's threw punches like medieval catapults
threw boulders.

Walking around at about two hundred thirty pounds and training down to two hundred twelve pounds during his prime, he was
by all reports exceptionally strong. George Foreman, who used to
spar with Liston in the late 1960s, said that he was the only man
ever able to move him backwards. Liston fought several large men.
He did not have to concede space.

Fifty years ago, big men trained down from their "walking
around" weight. Today, fewer heavyweights are so disciplined. They
seemed to have signed tacit agreements to waltz and posture rather
than wage war. They don't have to fight fifteen rounds anymore and
they barely bother breaking a sweat in twelve. Liston did, and as a
group, the men he fought came into the ring in good condition.

Liston's dimensions make him a juggernaut. Standing just under six feet one inch, he had the proportions of a larger man. His
musculature was streamlined and functional, and the veins popping
out of his neck looked like cables. His presence in the ring exuded a
bullish power, and his center of gravity, lower than longer men like

Lennox Lewis, translated into more concentrated physical strength. It is doubtful that any modern heavyweight would physically dominate Liston.

"When he hits," an acquaintance told Jack McKinney in 1962, "he hits every cop who ever beat him. He hits every white man who ever looked at him. I think he's on the edge of violence." Like Lennox and the Klitschkos, Liston could punch hard with either hand. Unlike Lennox or the Klitschkos, Liston's chin was rock solid.

His exceptional physical strength and punching power would serve him well against smaller champions like Dempsey, Marciano, and Frazier. Tyson admitted in the late eighties that he saw trouble with the Liston jab, but he'd have had more trouble coping with Liston's strength. Evander Holyfield's strategy against Tyson was grounded in the theory that Tyson's offense required forward motion. So Holyfield muscled him back and punched while Tyson was out of position. If Holyfield's relatively spindly legs could walk Tyson backwards, Liston would have no problem doing the same.

He would be hard to withstand for any of his heavyweight peers who couldn't match his strength. Those who could are very few. And even if a Foreman or a Klitschko could deal with his strength, they'd still have to find a way to overcome a surprising level of skill.

Technical Skill/Experience

Ali himself conceded that Liston's brutality was scientific. Liston was unusual in this regard. Joe Louis was arguably the supreme technician among the heavyweight champions, but Liston was at least as well-rounded as Larry Holmes, Tyson, Holyfield, or Riddick Bowe. He was a murderous body puncher, knew his way around at close quarters, was devastating at mid-range, and could control most fighters from outside. His jab was a telephone pole used not to dazzle, but to shock a man or knock him off balance so he could drive in with power shots.

Liston could punch in combination to the body and head. He could get a bit narcoleptic behind his jab, and he tended to follow movers like Clay and Eddie Machen instead of cutting the ring off. But when he cornered his man and bent those knees, his explosiveness could make a grown man cry. And the attack was intelligent. What he lacked in speed he compensated for with leverage, good balance, and shots that were short, diverse, and well-placed. This didn't change even as he aged. The punches he landed downstairs on Leotis Martin sounded like bowling balls dropping on wet salami.

Even at the end, Liston threw combinations that are noticeably absent among the punch-and-wait style of today's European giants. Left hooks were followed with right crosses, right crosses and uppercuts were followed by left hooks. Straight rights to the body were followed by left hooks to the head. He could adjust for distance and find angles. He did not disdain defense. His head moved after punching. He blocked, parried, weaved under shots, and got into position to return fire. At times Sonny's skillful slips and counters could make James Toney raise an eyebrow.

There are several heavyweight champions who faced better competition than Liston, though he did gain indispensable experience facing several different styles in a seventeen-year career, including boxer-punchers, counter-punchers, swarmers, sluggers, southpaws, and super heavyweights.

Intangibles

"When I broke his jaw," Marty Marshall recalled, "he didn't even blink." That was 1954, ten years before Liston met Clay. Cleveland Williams broke his nose in the first round of their first war in 1959. Blood poured like lava, but from the expression on Liston's face, it looked like he was playing poker. In the rematch, Williams stunned him in round two only to see Liston shut him down seconds later. Liston virtually cleaned out the top ten contenders on his way to Floyd Patterson.

How many fighters today would be willing to accept high risk/low reward bouts? Prime Liston built his ring reputation on exactly that.

In the end, it can be argued that Liston was a complete heavyweight. Most of the division's champions excelled with fewer assets than Liston. Like any fighter, he also had a stylistic foil. He had trouble with boxers who were fast and unorthodox. Marshall demonstrated this in his victory over Liston and Machen disrupted Liston's malevolent intentions by staying just outside the perimeter, turning him, and countering.

Angelo Dundee took notes and was convinced early that Cassius Clay had a surplus of essentials necessary to thwart Liston. Clay was tall, fast, mobile, and had more power and physical strength than either Marshall or Machen. Clay also forced Liston to turn and constantly reset and was smart enough to circle left—away from that big jab and left hook. In a peak-for-peak battle between 1959 Liston and 1967 Ali, Ali must be favored. He had the answers.

But there are no supermen. Ali himself was not immune to good strategy and stylistic kryptonite. Frazier's high pressure, bobbing and weaving style would always have been problematic for Ali. Ali needed room, had real limitations inside, and habitually dropped his right hand in time for Frazier's left hook. Tyson, who was essentially a gamma-powered Frazier, would also have been problematic for Ali. Marciano knew how to find his way inside and do heavy damage, though there is a good chance that Ali's corkscrew shots would have made marinara out of his face. If the contest discussed here included rematches, then Ali could be counted on to defeat anyone the second time if not the first. As it is, I would argue that his hypothetical record against his peers would place second.

Larry Holmes's style of fighting most resembles Ali's, but he had neither the speed of hand and foot nor the virtuosity of Ali. He was prone to punch wide and engage, and these would be mistakes against Liston. Holyfield had skills to match Liston, but he was prone to make the same mistake as Holmes by willingly engaging a superior offensive force. It is not likely that any of the champions would beat 1959 Liston by outgunning him. Those are his terms. Still more ominous is the high-tech know-how beneath the artillery.

Simply put, Liston may be too powerful for the skilled champions and too skilled for the powerful champions. To beat him, it takes a rare breed of heavyweight—the rarest, the Greatest.

Let us revisit the question: If the heavyweight kings of the modern era faced each other in their respective primes, who would have the best record? Who would be the king of the hill?

The shadow of Sonny Liston is emerging.

June 7, 2009

A Birthday for Sonny Liston

In the summer of 1962, Charles "Sonny" Liston and his wife Geraldine were living in the rectory of St. Ignatius Loyola in Denver, Colorado. Father Edward P. Murphy, the Jesuit who took them in, oversaw what the press was calling Sonny's "rehabilitation." The Jesuit preferred "reorientation"—a change of direction. The world's number-one ranked heavyweight contender had been suspended indefinitely in forty-seven states after yet another run-in with the law. He had good reason to change. He would rise at dawn to do roadwork at the City Park golf course and trained at a nearby Air Force base; weekends were spent at a Catholic retreat house in Fraser. Geraldine, who first met Sonny at a prison dance, said novenas for him at the church.

Father Murphy took it upon himself to teach his functionally-illiterate guest how to read, to heal some of the wounds on his personality. The wounds were old.

"We grew up like heathens," Sonny said. "When I was a kid, I had nothing but a lot of brothers and sisters, a helpless mother, and a father who didn't care about a single one of us." His mother's name was Helen, and she was about thirty years younger than his father, Tobin Liston. Tobin was the son of a slave who lived in Choctaw County, Mississippi and who can be found in the 1860 U.S. Census listed among the property of one Martin Liston. The Liston estate was valued at $6,825, which placed him far below the planter class.

Martin was just another small farmer who feared Abraham Lincoln and tended his cotton fields alongside four bent black people he wrongfully claimed as his own. Five years later "the freedom war" ended, and the 13th Amendment grew from Lincoln's grave like a blood-spattered rose.

By 1870, Alexander Liston was renting a plot of land not far from his former master's estate, now worth a paltry thousand dollars and owned by his widow.

Mississippi was not among the states that ratified the amendment. Resentment hovered in the thick, bleating air and before long slavery was revived in the form of a sharecropping system designed to keep freedmen in poverty. "The bossman got three-fourths of what you raised," Helen said. "We had to raise what we ate and then buy shoes and clothes."

There is no record of Alexander's feelings about this or anything else, but we know that his son was angry; the son of his son angrier still.

Tobin moved his family and elderly father northward to Johnson Township in St. Francis County, Arkansas. He was, by all reports, a man whose hostility could not be contained in the meager five-foot-five frame God had given him. It spilled out in torrents of abuse towards the oversized boy who didn't pick cotton fast enough and whose silence was mistook for a simple mind. Sonny wasn't sentimental about his childhood. "The only thing I ever got from my old man was a beating," he said.

Sonny, Father Murphy whispered, was "kicked around since he was born." Precisely how long that was has been a long-standing mystery because the date of his birth was never recorded. They rarely were in rural areas during the Depression, especially when it came to poor black folk, unless they did it themselves.

There was a tree on the farm in Arkansas where father and son toiled under a sun oblivious to change. Sonny spoke of it a few times. The birth dates of a new Liston generation were carved on that tree as if they had a right to hope. It was chopped down.

In 1950, Sonny was booked for robbery and told police he was born in 1928 or thereabouts. In 1953, he told Golden Gloves officials he was born in 1932 or thereabouts. During the Kefauver hearings in 1960, his massive shoulders strained his suit coat as he leaned into a microphone and said, "I was born in 1933." As champion, he chose May 8, 1932, as his default DOB to fend off the swarming press. They scoffed. His publicity man snapped, "He's over twenty-one." In the mid-sixties, when he was banned from fighting just about anywhere except Nevada and Sweden, Dan Daniel of THE RING said, "He doubtless is more than forty-five years of age." Before long the Swedish press joined the pestering chorus and Sonny got mad. Anyone, he started threatening, who doubted he was the age he claimed was calling his momma liar.

But momma only added to the confusion: "I think it was January 18th in 1932. I know he was born in January, in 1932. It was cold in January."

He eventually went and got himself a birth certificate, telling the clerk, the press, and his momma that he was born on May 8, 1932. He thought it would settle the matter. It didn't. A reporter who had befriended him named Jack McKinney revealed the sad truth. Sonny, he said, "was so sensitive on the issue of his age because he did not really know how old he was. When guys would write that he was thirty-two going on fifty, it had more of an impact on him that anybody realized. Sonny didn't know who he was."

He never would. What began with the crash of a felled tree in Arkansas ended on a night unknown, when a bench in his bedroom crashed under two hundred twenty pounds of dead weight. No one heard the tree fall. No one heard the bench crash. Both ends of his life, as loose and odd as expected, are tied up in a big black bow.

Why then does his story seem unfinished? Somewhere in the back of beyond, an enormous fist is still shaking, not with rage but with regret; the regret of not knowing.

We can look back now—way back—and perhaps provide solace to a ghost.

The 1940 U.S. Census reports have been released. Tobin Liston and his family come into view on a rented farm in backwater Smith Township on April 23, of that year. They moved there from backwater Johnson Township sometime between 1930 and 1934. Tobin is sixty-seven and working on the farm sixty hours a week despite his advanced age. Helen is minding the chores in and around the rented shack, and it's easy to conjure up a picture of her wiping her hands on an apron as she greets the census taker. It would have been her who gave the names and ages of the children: Leo ("17"), Annie ("15"), and Alcora ("13"), and there, between Curtis ("11") and Wesley ("2"), "Charles L" appears on record for the first time.

His age is given as "10," which means that 1930 is the likeliest year of his birth. However, Helen seemed prone to count the years from birth inclusively. A pointer is found in the 1930 census. On April 28, 1930, Curtis was listed at "6/12" months old (which strongly suggests that he was born in October 1929), and no child named Charles was listed in the Liston household. A decade later, Curtis was indeed in his eleventh year as his mother roughly claimed, though he was actually ten years old. Charles, then, was probably in his tenth year, though still nine years old.

If Curtis was born in October 1929, then Sonny's default birthday of May 8, can be put to the wind, barring the unlikely event that he survived a premature delivery in a shotgun shack in a backward county with no doctor in sight. It is almost certain that he was born no earlier than July 1930.

As time stretched away from that census taker's visit to the farm, Helen began to lose track. She was in her sixties when she said he was born in January—either January "8th" or "18th." Nick Tosches found that another sibling's birth was registered as January 8 and supposed that she mixed them up. Late in life, Helen rummaged through her memory again and said he was born in 1927. She seems to have confused the year of Sonny's birth with Alcora's, which was 1927. But there's another scrap of information, easily overlooked, that may end the mystery. Helen also said that Sonny was born on July 22.

Looking past her confusion about the year, we come face-to-face with a summer day that isn't easily explained away and that happens to fall within the allowable time frame for a viable pregnancy.

It fits. Perhaps a mother's memory can be counted on after all.

A birth date emerges out of the thick, bleating air of the Mississippi Delta. Its jagged script, barely legible anymore, is carved on a resurrected tree: 7-22-1930, Charles L.

August 31, 2012

THE GODS OF WAR

THE TEN GREATEST FIGHTERS
OF THE MODERN ERA

Series Introduction

I am the greatest!
—The Iliad, bk. XXIII, l. 746

Manny Pacquiao began his career in 1995 as an undernourished junior flyweight. Fourteen years and forty pounds later, he invaded the welterweight division after seizing the flyweight, featherweight, Junior lightweight, and Junior welterweight crowns. That's four crowns, not bogus belts. In September 2013, Floyd Mayweather took his own fourth crown against Saul "El Canelo" Alvarez—a bigger, stronger, natural puncher thirteen years his junior. Mayweather's masterful performance at the MGM Grand in Las Vegas reduced a hostile crowd of over 16,000 to silence. At the post-fight press conference, he wore a hat that said "TBE" ("The Best Ever").

Pacquiao and Mayweather are knocking on the gilded door of all-time distinction and a place for them will have to be prepared at the fistic table of the great and terrible. Legendary fighters, living and dead, are watching. Old boxing debates have reignited in a new media where millions have an instant platform to weigh in.

Their exposure is unprecedented. Their greatness is not. History has much to teach us.

The First Bell

The modern era of professional boxing can be traced back to a specific date. James J. Walker, a son of Irish immigrants and minority leader of the New York Senate, piloted a bill that legalized the sport statewide. The governor signed it on May 25, 1920. The "Walker Law" standardized weight divisions and sanctioned fights with official decisions rendered by a referee and judges. No longer would newspapers declare winners the morning after "exhibitions" of banned contests. The law also required all participants to be licensed, capped off the rounds at fifteen, instituted the neutral corner rule, placed a physician at ringside, attached penalties for intentional fouls, assigned five-ounce gloves for lightweights and lighter divisions and six-ounce gloves for the heavier divisions, and created the New York State Athletic Commission.

Promoter Tex Rickard wasted no time. He financed structural improvements to the old Madison Square Garden and staged six world title bouts in the first year after the law was enacted. New York became the Mecca of manly mayhem. Other states followed suit. In 1921, Jack Dempsey defended the heavyweight crown against Georges Carpentier in New Jersey and Rickard raked in the first million-dollar gate.

It was the Dollar Decade, the Age of Wonderful Nonsense, and prizefighting climbed up from the waterfront and hit the glitz. Booze was outlawed the same year that boxing went on the level but it didn't matter; the bluenoses were besieged in an era of shifting values. Jazz clubs sprang up and the Harlem Renaissance blossomed, young women bobbed their hair and stopped blushing. Post-war prosperity made the United States the richest country in the world, and when there is less to worry about, there is less to worry about. Everything happened fast—fast and loose—and the once sure line between the hill and the tenements, between black and white, between conventionality and criminality, got hazy.

The man most responsible for legalizing boxing became mayor of New York in 1926. "Beau James" was a dandy on the social scene and a politician only when he felt like it. Inevitably, Walker's failings ripened into corruption charges that forced his resignation. He fled to Europe on a cruise ship before returning a few years later to stage an unlikely comeback.

The story of boxing's modern era parallels the ups and downs of its godfather. Like Walker, it has been periodically exiled until the rousing cheers around a big event or a charismatic champion revitalize it. Like Walker, boxing is stark in its contrasts. Little wonder, then, that so many eminent writers celebrated it during the twentieth century; the prize ring is rife with poetry.

It is also rife with crime. The profiteers who have exploited it from the beginning have nothing poetic about them. Rich, fat, and easy to identify, today's profiteers come in assorted colors and are doing what any self-respecting hoodlum from the 1950s would consider perverse: They're killing the sport. Unchecked promoters turn their backs on public demand for match-ups unless they have options on both corners. So-called sanctioning bodies create unnecessary weight divisions and spawn sham titles to expand their influence and collect more fees. It's enough to wax nostalgic about the less-bad old days when Frankie Carbo was fixing fights in the shadow of Madison Square Garden.

Tweet this: In 1949, there were nine divisions with nine champions at the top of each one. As of this writing, the WBC, WBA, IBF, and WBO are putting the squeeze on seventeen divisions. Together they list seventy-seven different champions defending eighty-four title belts and paying each respective organization for the honor. The sanctioning bodies are defecating on the once-regal concept of "champion."

If you want to find boxing, you'll find it where your grandfather usually found it—down and out in the gutter of Jimmy Cannon's red-light district. The boxer himself is there too, but he's standing up like he always has.

And isn't that what it's all about?

Split Decisions

The idea of boxing remains as pure as the idea of bravery. It remains as compelling as any collision with something at stake. It stirs questions. One of them is the definitive question that echoes across the district and down generations: which among those who followed Virgil's ancient exhortation to "lace on the gloves and put up his hands" are the greatest?

The debates never end. Media outlets and respected organizations such as ESPN, the Associated Press, THE RING, and the International Boxing Research Organization have weighed in. Everyone who is anyone has offered their own pound-for-pound pecking orders at one time or another, though they're usually too flawed to take seriously. Most pundits today, for example, came of age in the sixties and seventies and rank the self-proclaimed "Greatest" at the very top. Muhammad Ali has become their saint—sanitized, secularized, and puffed-up. He represents baby-boomers, before the paunch. He must be the greatest; even if he isn't.

Insiders who have been around for decades can't be counted on either. In his all-time top-ten list, the late Angelo Dundee included not one but four fighters he trained: Ali, Ray Leonard, Luis Rodriguez, and George Foreman. Others confuse the point of the whole exercise. Instead of surveying accomplishments, they imagine each boxer in the same weight class and speculate as to which would win had two of them fought.

Bill Gray's *Boxing's Top 100: The Greatest Champions of All Time* stomps on the stogie of folk wisdom and throws a sponge at unreliable subjective opinion. Gray applied scientific rigor in a commendable effort to rank seven-hundred champions active since 1882. Each champion was scored relative to his peers in four areas of comparison: Age, Years, Title Bouts, and Career Bouts.

However, the rankings suffer because a high number of bouts and wins were not sifted by scrutinizing the quality of opposition. A record built on Hall of Famers is indistinguishable from one built on cab drivers. Additionally, bogus belts are counted as authentic world championships and history's uncrowned champions are completely ignored. At times, the results boggle the mind. After his mathematics placed Joe Gans ten spots behind Virgil Hill, a great muffled guffaw was heard from Nat Fleischer's grave.

The cold hard fact is that it takes more than cold hard facts to understand something so dynamic. Boxing is about sweat and blood. Understanding it requires getting close enough to see it splattered on your shirt, if not leaking out of your face. A definitive list, then, would come with objective data in one hand and a glove on the other.

This series will present just such a definitive list.

Forget the rest. Expect the unexpected and resist the urge to make assumptions because no boxer, regardless of how sacred his name, was given a boost. Worth keeping in mind is that the actual number of great fighters is obviously far larger than ten, so if your favorite wasn't up to that scratch, check the appendix for the next twenty. If he doesn't appear there either, understand that it doesn't mean he isn't "great"; it merely suggests that there are others still greater.

The greater ones share common features: Razor-sharp trainers stood behind them. They tended to climb out of conditions that were apparent in the United States during those three decades after the Walker Law (between 1920 and 1950), when hard men had fewer options outside of the prize ring and were paid just enough to compel them to fight hordes of other hard men. As a result, they were sifted by experience to become proven quantities.

Two parameters are necessary. First, fighters active before the Walker Law were considered only if they had reached their peak after 1920. This excludes Bob Fitzsimmons, Packey McFarland, Sam Langford, and Jimmy Wilde, among others. Brilliant though they were, they were representatives of a different era when boxing was essentially a different sport. The second parameter requires that only those fighters retired for at least five years be considered. Smoke must clear before we can draw informed conclusions about a career.

The Criteria:
1. *Quality of Opposition* (maximum 25 points):
This category is the most important measure of greatness.

The number and frequency of International Boxing Hall of Famers, true world champions, and serious threats appearing on the fighter's record are examined.

2. *Ring Generalship* (maximum 15 points):
How effective a fighter was at controlling the flow of battle reflects ring generalship. "Control" may be established through advanced technique, natural assets/athleticism, and by imposing the will.

3. *Longevity* (maximum 15 points):
Length of career and number of fights at the world-class level matter here. Fighters with less than fifty professional bouts should not be expected to score high in this category. Significant post-prime wins also matter here.

4. *Dominance* (maximum 15 points):
This category examines the number of wins against losses and the length of championship reigns or winning streaks for those routinely avoided.

5. *Durability* (maximum 10 points):
It's tough to put a good man down and even tougher to keep him there. Only "due credit" is applied here. For example, those fighters who were never or rarely stopped but faced few punchers during their career should not be expected to receive the highest scores. The same may apply to those defensive technicians rarely touched.

6. *Performance against Larger Opponents* (maximum 10 points).
The natural disadvantage of facing a larger opponent forces the smaller man to demonstrate something beyond what he would when facing a man his own size. A win over a larger opponent can be compelling evidence of just how good that fighter was.

7. *Intangibles* (maximum 10 points)
Boxing is a character sport first. Most top fighters will score fairly

high in this category. Unusual risks taken, adversity overcome, and resilience are a few of the qualities examined here.

Categories such as "Mainstream Appeal" or "Contributions to the Sport of Boxing" have no bearing here, despite their unfortunate usage in popular rankings. They are based on charisma and political forces and have nothing at all to do with how great a boxer was as a boxer. This isn't a popularity contest, after all. "Head-to-Head" determinations are not included either because they are too speculative.

The sweet science as we know it has the seasoning of a century behind it. There are legends in its dusty volumes, legends reanimated and examined by those of us who won't let them rest. Consider this your official program. Ten men you may or may not be familiar with will be summoned from a literary dressing room in ascending order. They will take a bow and then take a throne. The countdown will conclude with the emergence of the preeminent fighter of the modern era—the *ne plus ultra*, "the god of war."

Now the spotlight falls center-ring. A silver-coiffed announcer stands there as a microphone lowers from the rafters.

In his hand are ten scorecards.

Serpentine stylist. Uncrowned champion. Giant killer.
(Courtesy of Harry Otty)

The Tenth God of War

$\mathbf{T}$*he evening sun is sinking over the Oakland section of Pittsburgh, Pennsylvania like a great red fist. An old man sits in a wheelchair on a front porch. There's a scrapbook on his lap under large hands gnarled by years of work and war. Melancholy eyes begin to close behind glasses as the man nods off. The pages of his life come alive during these twilight dreams, and for a few moments he is burning with youth again, strong again, walking the avenue in a long coat with a cocked Stetson hat and Florsheim shoes. "Hey champ," ghosts from the past say as he saunters by.*

He was never the champ, but the whole city knows he should have been, would have been, had he only been given a chance.

Fight films click on in his head.

"I Just Wanted to Fight . . ."

Elmer "Violent" Ray stood six feet two inches, weighed two hundred pounds, and wrestled alligators in Florida for fun. With arms like bazookas, he hit hard enough to be counted among THE RING's "100 Greatest Punchers of All Time."

In 1946, Ray would drive heavyweight contender Lee Savold into the canvas like a tent stake, and as a result, he was given a wide field to graze by himself. For years, Joe Louis wouldn't even get in the ring with him for an exhibition.

But a certain welterweight from Pittsburgh did. Despite the fact that he stood only five feet nine inches and weighed little more than a hundred and fifty pounds between fights, he agreed to spar with Ray when both were training at the Main Street Gym in Los Angeles.

Witnesses said that Ray proceeded to do what he always did—he hurled his bulk at his opponent as if his mother's dignity depended on it. Witnesses also said that every shot he threw was slipped. Frustrated, Ray sought to impose his will by shoving the welterweight through the ropes and onto the ring apron, where he landed with a thud. With that, heavy bags suddenly stopped jumping on chains, speed bags stuttered to a stop, and skip ropes dropped to the floor as a small crowd of fighters drifted over. Trainers spat and chuckled as the welterweight climbed back into the ring.

They knew what was coming next.

The heavyweight didn't. He thought he had him now.

Stomping forward, he launched a big right hand; but it missed and the welterweight landed his own right, followed by a left hook, and Elmer Ray crashed down to take an involuntary mid-afternoon nap, mid-ring.

Ray posted big wins over name fighters and became the world's number-one ranked heavyweight contender in early 1947, but if anyone asked him who hit him the hardest, his answer was always the same: a welterweight by the name of *Charley Burley*.

Shaken, Not Stirred

The first crown Charley Burley went after was affixed to the head of the great Henry Armstrong. Armstrong's management reportedly told Burley that he would not get a shot at the welterweight title because Armstrong was moving back down to the lightweight division. It wasn't true. Armstrong would make a record number of welterweight defenses, and Burley would never get a shot. Fellow Pittsburgher Fritzie Zivic, who lost to Burley twice and was ranked behind him, got the shot. Zivic took the title and then went to comedic lengths to avoid facing Burley again—he bought Burley's contract. Only after he lost the title did he sell the contract to Tommy O'Loughlin for $500. Zivic's successor, Freddie "Red" Cochrane declined to fight Burley despite the fact that Burley offered to fight him for free.

Early in 1942, the *Pittsburgh Post-Gazette* reported that O'Loughlin wired an offer of $7500 to the manager of light heavyweight champion Billy Conn for a fight with Burley in Minneapolis. The offer was laughed at. Conn might have remembered those early sparring sessions in Pittsburgh that were the talk of the black community. Middleweights were no braver. There was a persistent rumor that Marcel Cerdan considered facing Burley when he arrived to the American shore, but after watching him beat up on his sparring partners, he lost interest.

Burley was forced to contend for frivolous titles, like the so-called "colored" middleweight title and the middleweight title of California, where he faced fighters almost as great and just as forgotten as he is. Public challenges were unmet, phone calls unanswered, and managers went deaf the moment his name was uttered.

"I'd go anywhere to fight anybody," he said when he was old. "If they'd get somebody for me I'd fight them. I just wanted to fight . . . I knew I could have held my own against anybody—that's the God's truth." O'Loughlin took that at face value. He figured that if the iron of three divisions wouldn't face Burley, perhaps the giants would.

To really turn heads, O'Loughlin decided to pit Burley against a heavyweight journeyman named JD Turner, who had just gone the distance with Conn. After obtaining permission from the Athletic Commission of Minnesota to fight Turner, based on the reasoning that Burley was having difficulty finding willing opponents in his own weight class, Burley climbed through the ropes to face a man who was a half-foot taller and sixty-eight pounds heavier. It was a physical mismatch and a novelty. It was also a rout.

In the opening seconds, Burley landed a right cross that crossed the eyes and rattled the teeth of Turner. The *Post-Gazette* reported that from that moment to the end of the sixth round, Burley was "his master, punching and batting the big Texan at will." Turner didn't answer the bell for the seventh round. "That little sucker," he said, "—knocked me cold. I woke up in the dressing room."

A week later, O'Loughlin walked into the Pennsylvania Boxing Commission to get another waiver. Burley, ranked fourth in the welterweight division, was looking for a fight against six feet four inches of Harry Bobo, a third-ranked heavyweight whose nickname was "The Paralyzer."

The Wild West

Nothing came of that, so he went west where the wild things were. In the 1940s, California was the scene of an alternative boxing universe where Burley would join a group of African American fighters at constant war with each other. Budd Schulberg would later remember them as "that murderers' row of Negro middleweights carefully avoided by the titleholders." All told, there were eight of them, and they faced each other sixty-two times. Burley came out of their round-robin tournaments with the best record, going 11-5-1 with one no-contest. Notoriously tough and durable, none of them managed to win by knockout more than once in bouts against the others—except for Burley, who scored three.

Sugar Ray Robinson was no more eager than any other champion to face these fighters, but he did use Cocoa Kid and Aaron "Little Tiger" Wade as sparring partners in the late 1940s. Wade was semi-retired when he separated Robinson's ribs in 1948. Inactive at thirty-five years old, Cocoa Kid dropped a peaking Sugar Ray in the summer of 1949. This occurred after Robinson was accused of breaking an agreement to fight him in April.

In the early forties, a young Ray Robinson was himself an avoided prospect, so Tommy O'Loughlin tried to set up an eliminator between Robinson and Burley. No dice. "Sugar Ray would never fight him," O'Loughlin recounted in 1981. "I know. I tried to make the match several times."

Burley defeated Little Tiger Wade, a puncher, in March 1944. He then faced Jack Chase, an experienced speed demon who was called "Young Joe Louis" early in his career. Burley didn't like cocky fighters like Chase. Paul Lowry of the *Los Angeles Times* watched Chase miss with his jab repeatedly while Burley snaked and weaved before landing a series of consecutive rights that felled him flat on his face. Chase hadn't been knocked out in over seven years.

Burley had by then settled in San Diego and was working in an aircraft factory when he got the call to face Archie Moore. Moore was at least as cocky as Chase and perhaps to make a point, Burley barely trained. Early in the first round, Moore was stretched on the canvas, thinking that Burley had a lug wrench in his right glove. He went down three more times in rounds three, four, and eight—the last time by a jab. Moore's famous cross-armed defense was easily solved by Burley's straight right hands, which closed Moore's eye and swelled up the left side of his face. Moore was amazed: "He outboxed me," he said. "That's something I couldn't understand, because nobody had ever done that before."

An added insult came on the wings of gossip. Moore heard that Burley was playing cards and drinking whiskey the night before the bout.

Like many other great fighters of the forties, Burley would have whirlwind campaigns where he would fight several serious opponents in a short span of time. Compare this to today's version of greatness. Consider Manny Pacquiao in 2008. Pacquiao defeated Juan Manuel Marquez in March, David Diaz in June, and Oscar De La Hoya in December. The weight jumping is impressive, but Burley would fight giants without gaining a pound. Pacquiao took three good scalps and had a great year, but he also had three and a half months and five months off between them. Burley beat up Archie Moore fifteen days after knocking out Jack Chase, and he knocked out Chase thirteen days after outpointing Little Tiger Wade. Defeating three great fighters inside of five weeks is the mark of a complete fighter.

Some said he was a perfect fighter.

By the time he unwrapped his hands for the last time and hung up the gloves, he had been openly avoided by at least four champions in three divisions. In a ninety-eight-bout career that began in 1936 and ended in 1950, he faced down five of his peers in the International Boxing Hall of Fame, including Moore, Fritzie Zivic, Billy Soose, and two members of Murderers' Row in Holman Williams and Cocoa Kid.

And despite the monsters he faced—the bangers, the speed demons, the technicians, and the giants, he was never stopped.

". . . Never stopped," a dozing Charley Burley murmurs as film clutter splays in his mind, and a sound like a rattling projector rouses him. A car drags a tailpipe as it passes by his front porch. The old man wipes his eyes and returns to the present, to the familiar hum of traffic on Penn Lincoln Parkway, to the cool evening breeze. Street lights announce that the red sun has gone down to defeat, though tomorrow will see it rise again. There's reassurance in that. In a moment, the screen door will open and Julia will bring a blanket for his lap.

One of boxing's greatest uncrowned champions looks to the darkening sky with hope, and then looks down at his hands . . . and clenches a fist.

CHARLEY BURLEY'S SCORECARD

—25 points—
Quality of Opposition: 24.3

—15 points—
Ring Generalship: 14.5
Longevity: 13.2
Dominance: 12.5

—10 points—
Durability: 10
P/LO: 9.4
Intangibles: 9.7

Total *93.6*

The Will o' the Wisp circa 1947, the greatest defensive boxer in history. (Press Photo)

The Ninth God of War

He was the best boxer I ever saw.
—Sugar Ray Robinson

Stillman's Gym was founded in 1921, not one year after the New York State Legislature passed James J. Walker's landmark bill legalizing boxing. Legend has it that Benny Leonard led a troupe of Jewish fighters out of Grupp's Gym after Billy Grupp got drunk and blamed Jews for everything from the war to the weather. According to trainer Ray Arcel, Stillman's didn't start out as a boxing gym, though it became one for two reasons: First, a throng of admirers frequently followed Leonard into the gym to watch him train. Second, manager Lou Ingber was no fool. He charged admission.

By the 1940s, Lou Ingber had changed his name to Lou Stillman for simplicity's sake. Jack Curley sat at the door collecting fifty cents a head. The "modest entrance," A.J. Liebling recounted, "is the kind of hallway you would duck into if you wanted to buy marijuana in a strange neighborhood." The gym was open from noon to four every day, including Christmas. Fight fans of all shapes and sizes came in: shifty-eyed characters chewing toothpicks, high school students playing hooky, ex-pugs with nowhere else to go. Every day a hundred or more would walk up a wide wooden stairway to the main floor as two rings came into view and bass lines reverberated from speed bags like precursors to hip hop records. Sweat, liniment, and cigarette smoke filled the air, and fifteen rows were set up for spectators to watch the greatest array of champions ever assembled in one place.

Stillman was no sweetheart. "Big or small, champ or bum," he said, "I treated 'em all the same way—bad." Charles Dickens described Ebenezer Scrooge as "a squeezing, wrenching, grasping, scraping, clutching, covetous old sinner," but Stillman didn't need no stinkin' scribbler to describe him. He described himself as "a grouch, a crab, a cranky guy who never smiled." And he did better than Scrooge; he justified it with a .38 caliber pistol he carried in plain sight. No one was spared his bad disposition, not the connected managers or the wise guys they were connected to.

Almost no one.

One of the fighters training at Stillman's was a wisp of an Italian who smiled often and razzed anyone for a laugh, especially himself. He had more trouble at home with his wife, he would say, than he had in almost any of his two hundred and forty-one career bouts. History would crown him the greatest defensive boxer who ever lived.

"Stillman loved me," he recalled years later.

On November 20, 1942, Madison Square Garden was filled to the rafters. Chalky Wright, thirty, was recognized by the New York State Athletic Commission as the world featherweight champion when he stepped into the ring for his third defense. Bouncing on his toes across the ring was the Italian, ten years his junior. Due to age restrictions, the kid had to lie to boxing officials to get a title shot, he told them he was twenty-one. An unruly contingent of paisans from Harford filled half the arena, shouting curses Chalky's way. When the first bell clanged, the young challenger sprinted out of his corner to center ring, put his dukes up . . . and disappeared. He spent round after round fighting like a figment of Wright's imagination, offering only mirages in lieu of mayhem like a laughing ghost.

This was the artistry of "Will o' the Wisp" the *nom de guerre* of Willie Pep. A will o' the wisp is a mysterious light or a mischievous spirit that was believed to lead English travelers onto false paths. Pep preferred "Will o' the Wop."

According to the *New York Times*, Wright was forced to "hold his fire through most of the battle to avoid appearing ludicrous as Pep stuck and stabbed and broke and ran." Wright the puncher became Wright the plodder. He was peppered with stinging lefts and rights while his counter punches sailed windily over curly hair and narrow shoulders. For the first four rounds it seemed that the only peril for Pep was catching a cold from the draft.

In the fifth, sixth, and seventh rounds, Wright caught up and pummeled him on the ropes. In the ninth round, he launched a right cross and Pep ducked and caught it on the top of his head. "This guy punched so hard that he could hit you on top of your head and daze you," remembered Pep, "and I've got a pretty hard head." Pep surprised everyone when he took over again before the end of the round, planting his feet to turn and outslug the champion. Both judges and the referee saw Wright win only four of the fifteen rounds.

Willie Pep became the new featherweight champion of the whole wide woild—at least in New York.

Four years and forty-seven fights later, Pep stopped Sal Bartolo in the twelfth round to take the National Boxing Association's world featherweight title. Then the champion shattered any illusions that the legendary Manuel Ortiz had about standing taller than a bantamweight, and defeated Wright three more times. The last time he faced the ex-champion, he ended his misery in three rounds. "Willie," Wright said afterwards. "I had enough of you. I give up."

In January 1947, Pep climbed a set of stairs that very nearly turned out to be a stairway to heaven. He was a passenger on a tin can flight from Miami to Hartford during a snowstorm. The plane crashed near Millville, New Jersey, and three passengers were killed. The featherweight champion, his left leg snapped like a twig and his back broken in two places, woke up in a hospital bed with three quarters of his frame in cast. Pep was lucky to be alive and few had any illusions that he'd fight again. The master of illusions himself was not about to let this one master him: "I'm through," he said.

"I'm through flying at night!"

In June, he was back in the ring. In July, he fought five times. On October 29, 1948, he stepped through the ropes with a record that shined like no boxer's record ever will again. Willie Pep was 134-1-1.

Sandy Saddler loomed over the champion like a telephone poll over a truant, and that dazzling record didn't even constrict his pupils. His record of 85-6-2 with sixty-three knockouts was the mark of a true puncher and Pep had no idea what he was in for. Neither did the bookies. Saddler, a three-to-one underdog, ignored Pep's feints, spins, and set-ups, and zeroed in on every fleeting glimpse and fading shadow in that ring that wasn't wearing a bow tie. Pep was knocked out in four rounds. "Out—" said Saddler. It was Archie Moore who designed the blueprint for victory. And he did it at Stillman's Gym. "He wanted me to stay on top of him and give him no leverage," Saddler told Peter Heller.

Pep's trainer was Bill Gore of Providence, Rhode Island. This was the man who took not only the natural athleticism but also the nervous energy of a teenage Guglielmo Papaleo and built a foundation of skill underneath it. Pep was a savant. Gore was the strategist behind him, watching films, analyzing Saddler's nightmare style, and devising a plan to win the rematch.

That rematch is considered one of the greatest fights of the twentieth century. Pep, only three years removed from a ghost ride in the sky and four months removed from a devastating knockout, followed orders. Ringsiders at Madison Square Garden watched the odds-on favorite eat thirty-seven consecutive jabs in the first round. Saddler was a "baffled and bewildered" slugger reduced to shadow boxing. However, his long arms were like whips and whips can take a cigarette out of a mouth at twelve feet if handled by an expert. Saddler managed to cut Willie below his left eye, and above and below his right eye. In the fourth round, he landed a straight left; in the ninth, a straight right; in the tenth, a right to the jaw that had Pep reeling. In the fourteenth, it was a left hook, then another right. Pep somehow shook it off and "gave no quarter . . . pelting Saddler with every blow known to boxing." In the last round, it was Pep who was "fighting Saddler all over the ring."

It was the greatest triumph of his career. It remains one of the greatest triumphs in boxing history.

Thanksgiving Day 2006, Rocky Hill, Connecticut. In a room at the West Hill Convalescent Home, Willie Pep finally kept still long enough for mortality to land a shot. His mischievous spirit emerged from a body stooped with age, and climbed a stairway.

The stairway was not the familiar four steps leading into a boxing ring, nor did it lead into a plane like the one he boarded sixty years earlier.

It was a golden one, as brilliant as the belt he wore for so long, so long ago.

It was a wide one, wider than that wooden stairway headed up to a certain gym in the New York City of his dreams.

It was a stairway lined with many who departed before him—more than a few ex-wives, two great featherweight rivals he never forgot, and the curmudgeon who loved him, Lou Stillman.

WILLIE PEP'S SCORECARD

—25 points—
Quality of Opposition: 24

—15 points—
Ring Generalship: 15
Longevity: 14.8
Dominance: 14.9

—10 points—
Durability: 8.2
P/LO: 7.5
Intangibles: 9.4
Total *93.8*

When the best fighters in the world were Jewish, the Ghetto Wizard was the best of the best. (Courtesy of Don Cogswell)

The Eighth God of War

To be a Jew is a destiny.
—Hedwig Baum

The Jews of medieval Spain were famous for their fencing skills. Fencing, like boxing, evolved out of brutal origins into a sport that retained its aggressiveness but added a measure of gentility. The fencer salutes his opponent. The boxer extends a glove. The combatants in both sports engage one another under a clear set of rules to show dominance, and the similarities do not end there. Fencing relies on foreknowledge. A fencer will look for patterns in his opponent's reactions and then invite a reaction with the idea of countering it with an effective thrust. The boxer does the same. Competing well in either sport relies on reaction time, agility, coordination, and self-confidence. The ability to mount an attack while being acutely aware of defense is critical. Strategy is critical.

Legend has it that a bare-knuckle boxer from the eighteenth century named Daniel Mendoza (1763-1836) was descended from those Jewish fencers and incorporated some of their theories into his fighting style. What is more certain is that the bullish man with the curly black hair who preferred to be announced as "Mendoza the Jew" was a true pioneer of the sweet science. He helped redefine it as a thinking man's sport by operating behind a jab, sidestepping, and blocking to compensate for his relatively short stature. In an era where fighters had more cauliflower ears than eyebrows, his revolutionary style was refined, even graceful.

Like a stone tossed into history's pond, his influence rippled across a century into the golden era of Jewish-American boxing.

And what an era it was. Between 1910 and 1940, there were twenty-seven world champions of Hebrew descent. At the end of the Roaring Twenties, a time when boxing was a major sport and clubs were everywhere, fighters with names like Goldstein and Schwartz dominated the ranks. Many of them came out of the Lower East Side of Manhattan, the rough-and-tumble sons of immigrants who had poured in from Eastern Europe during the 1880s clinging to hope and carrying mezuzahs. Their parents had fled persecution. They fled from nobody.

One of them lived on Eighth Street, the son of a garment presser.

There was nothing intimidating about the appearance of the man born Benjamin Leiner. Standing only five feet five inches with features that could be considered handsome in a delicate sort of way, he called to mind David strumming a lyre more than he did the Samson-like Mendoza. As the proud product of a culture that frowned on prizefighting, he hid his profession from his parents out of respect. But he would not hide his identity. Jews beamed when they saw the familiar six-pointed star emblazoned on his trunks. In time, he became more than a champion.

He became Benny Leonard, the "Great Bennah," "the Ghetto Wizard," the *Shayner Yid* who convinced many gray heads under prayer shawls to embrace the muscular Judaism of the prize ring.

July 5 1920, Benton Harbor. The fifth round was underway and the twenty-four-year-old Leonard had his hands full with Charley White, a hard-punching veteran with a record of 73-9-4.

Leonard delivered an immaculate left jab to the head of his charging opponent, who responded with a right hook followed by four more rights to the face. All those rights were a set-up. While Leonard was roughly lulled into expecting another right, a left hook slammed into his chin. The champion fell through the ropes to the ring apron. The *Chicago Daily Tribune* reported that the dazed boxer couldn't get up because his legs were "dangling over the lower ropes while his shoulders reclined outside the hemp." The referee counted to four before Leonard's corner men pushed him back into the ring, where White climbed all over him like a cheap suit.

At the end of the eighth round, White was ahead on the score-cards. Leonard was making calculations. He was gauging White's biggest weapon, his left hook, so he could make it work against him. The ninth round began with what the *New York Times* called a light exchange. Leonard, biding his time, already had his eureka moment. It was simple geometry; specifically, a line inside an arc. When he saw White setting up to throw his left hook, Leonard quick-stepped inside of it and fired a straight right hand. White teetered and col-lapsed to his hands and knees. Like a good yeshiva student he got right back up, but the rabbi threw a sequence of textbook shots and sent him sprawling again.

White got up at the count of eight, and was then sent through the ropes as Leonard shook off a grudge he'd been nursing.

It was a thoroughly beaten man who climbed back into the ring. Another right welcomed him. Down he went. Up he got. The fifth time he went down, he got comfortable. His left arm, so fearsome only moments earlier, lay inert on the canvas. It was the first time White was counted out in his fifteen-year career.

The arena went wild. According to the *Times*, barriers were torn down and seats were broken as a mass of humanity pushed its way toward the ring. Several spectators were trampled, and the police could not hold back the crowd from the champion's corner. Leonard was forced to stand in the ring for almost a half-hour receiving the hearty handshakes and congratulations of a multitude.

February 10, 1922, Madison Square Garden. Leonard's nose was bleeding in the fourth round. Worse than that, his hair was mussed up. To a man known for his primping vanity, this was downright rude. Rocky Kansas, an Italian slugger out of Buffalo, New York, was landing big shots in an all-out effort to take the lightweight throne. Leonard was making his seventh defense of that throne but was fighting Kansas on Kansas's terms. As the fourth round ticked by, Leonard was visibly weakening under the strain, and Kansas encouraged his decline by battering his body in clinches and throwing haymakers at range. Leonard's sharpshooting skills were on display anyway, as he countered Kansas with short lefts to the stomach. It was a thrilling slugfest.

By the eleventh, the tide was turning. The investment downstairs was taking a toll on Kansas, and his neck was stretching like an accordion from constant jabs. Kansas went down for a count of nine after absorbing a right over the heart. When he got up, Leonard stepped in for the finishing touches. According to the *Los Angeles Times*, he "worked around the Italian like a cooper around a barrel, nailing him with lefts to face and body."

Leonard took the decision after fifteen rounds. The two would meet again five months later, only this time Kansas, a 2010 International Boxing Hall of Fame inductee, would not see the final bell.

"He whipped, he whipped me," he would say after he was stopped, "and oh can he hit."

The Southpaw

In July 1923, color-coordinated searchlights were installed at Yankee Stadium to direct the crowd to the different subway transit lines. Benny Leonard-Lew Tendler II marked the first time in history that such a lighting system was used for boxing after dark. With nearly 65,000 seats sold, that lightweight championship bout commanded the largest crowd since Jack Dempsey fought Georges Carpentier in Jersey City in 1921. Twenty dollars got you ringside. Leonard was a two-to-one favorite over a Philadelphian challenger widely considered the other best lightweight on the planet. The challenger had one distinct advantage—an alarming one.

Lew Tendler was a southpaw.

From the first moments that breed crawled backward out of the

THE GODS OF WAR

primordial ooze, campaigns have erupted against them. And why not? The English word "sinister" is derived from the Italian "sinistra" which means "from the left" or "evil." There is something unnatural about them. They're mirror images of the right-handed population, operating like Bizarro configurations that do everything wrong.

To be sure, the left-handed among us may argue that it could just as well be the right-handed who are mirror images for them, but we live in a democracy where majority rules, and it's a right-handed world.

Need proof? Watch a southpaw write with a ballpoint pen. They don't pull it across the page; they push it, and smudge ink all over their hands. They put belts on upside down. And they can be downright dangerous. Congress should ban them from handling sharp items never designed for them, such as scissors. Prefer blood on your bread? Ask one to cut the loaf. And if you see a left-hander in the cockpit of heavy machinery—run for your life.

Boxing managers recognize the danger. "Them southpaws," jibed Jim Wicks, "should be drowned at birth." For decades a left-handed novice would be converted to the conventional stance. Some trainers still do, although most have come to appreciate southpaw advantages.

Approximately twelve percent of the world's population is left-handed. This means that southpaws are far more acclimated to sparring with conventional boxers than conventional boxers are to sparring with southpaws. They confuse conventional fighters because their attack comes from opposite angles, and there are those who would argue that they are inherently stronger. Southpaw Manny Pacquiao may be the greatest fighter in the first decade of the twenty-first century, but it was Lew Tendler who was the quite possibly the best southpaw of the twentieth.

Benny Leonard's own prejudices may have been on display over those few years that Tendler had to wait for a title shot. Public clamor grew to fever pitch before the champion finally agreed to meet him in Philadelphia, but that bout was cancelled after Leonard broke a bone in his hand during training. Tendler promptly took the $5,000 forfeit put up by both fighters as a guarantee to show up and fight. Leonard demanded that the money be returned and was rebuffed. Tendler's manager then propped Tendler up as an alternative claimant to the lightweight throne without consulting the man who had kept the seat warm since 1917.

Tendler became a mirror image of Leonard with a sinister crown, and the Bizarro world of the southpaw was writ large.

Leonard and Tendler first met in the summer of 1922. It was a rude introduction. Tendler crossed a left onto Leonard's right eyebrow in the opening round and blood streamed. Leonard's shellacked hair was a disaster in no time at all, and his face would soon resemble a child's finger-painting. Before it was over, he'd be missing a tooth too.

The second round was Tendler's.

The third round was Tendler's.

By the fourth round Benny was wishing that boxing, like polo, would ban lefties from the sport altogether.

Eventually, inevitably, Leonard started solving the puzzle. He began finding the range with lead rights—a foil of backward boxers, and stepping around Tendler to force him to reset. Tendler, who also happened to be one of the greatest body-punchers in history, decried that progress by sinking a deep left into the stomach. Ringsiders heard Leonard gasp.

The fifth round was Tendler's.

Tendler took the eighth round after landing a left to the head that made Leonard's knees sag. The champion clinched, spun him, angled off, and threw shots as if he could still see straight. Reporters heard laughing in the clinch. It was another indication that Leonard was a *yiddisher kop*; he was talking to the fierce man in front of him, cutting jokes and making remarks to convince Tendler of the lie that he wasn't hurt. He was heard talking to Tendler in the ninth round as well, bluffing to buy time.

As the bell clanged for round ten, Leonard smiled and those at ringside saw a gap where a front tooth had been earlier.

Most observers had the champion only slightly ahead after twelve rounds. Some saw it as a draw. It was a no-decision bout, which meant that Tendler had to knock the champion out to take the title. He didn't. Leonard admitted that even his royal boxing I.Q. was almost not enough. "Southpaws are hard to solve," he said. "I found difficulty in solving Tendler's style from the outset."

The rematch, held under the new blue and white lights of Yankee Stadium on July 24, 1923, was a fifteen-round title bout. Babe Ruth was among those cheering at ringside. He witnessed how great a slugger Leonard was and watched him leave the ring with barely a mark on his face as a crowd gathered and hoisted him up onto shoulders. "Tendler," Leonard remarked after the victory, "is the greatest southpaw and one of the greatest lightweights I have ever seen." The southpaw also had something to say. It was as sincere as the cut over his eye and the pulp of his nose:

"Benny," he said, "is a master ring general."

With that tribute resounding in the ears of fight fans everywhere, the champion ended his seven-year reign over a fearsome division with a wink and a smile.

The stone that Daniel Mendoza tossed into history's pond generated a small army of great Jewish fighters in the opening stanzas of the twentieth century. Charley White and Lew Tendler were in those ranks. But it was Benny Leonard who ascended higher than them all, higher than just about any ring general who ever lived, ultimately reaching a place where the brilliance of the Star of David shined upon him, and he upon it.

BENNY LEONARD'S SCORECARD

—25 points—
Quality of Opposition: 24.3

—15 points—
Ring Generalship: 15
Longevity: 14.7
Dominance: 15

—10 points—
Durability: 8.7
P/LO: 8.2
Intangibles: 9.6

Total *95.5*

The Toy Bulldog (left) attacks Jack Sharkey, 1931.
(Rogers Photo Archive)

The Seventh God of War

It's not the size of the dog in the fight, but the size of the fight in the dog. —Mark Twain

Mickey Walker was born with a pug nose. He was a "throwback from the old breed of game," said journalist Westbrook Pegler, "fighting Irish who fought for hours and days and weeks with anything at hand merely to see which was the better man."

The man called "Toy Bulldog" was all of twenty-one years old when he challenged Jack Britton for the world welterweight crown at Madison Square Garden in 1922. Britton was fighting professionally when Mickey was still wearing a propeller on his cap, and only five months earlier had given the great Benny Leonard a boxing lesson.

But Britton won no more than three rounds against Mickey. He was forced to pay homage to conquering youth, taking a knee nearly six times. Before the decision was announced Britton walked over to the opposite corner to congratulate the new champion. "I wish you luck, boy," he said.

The victor was smiling from ear to ear as if he had shamrocks in his socks. He usually did.

After four defenses against welterweights, he jumped up two divisions to outclass light heavyweight champion Mike McTigue, and then bit off more than even a bulldog could chew when he faced middleweight champion Harry Greb six months later and lost a decision. Mickey retreated back to the welterweight division and licked his wounds. Exactly six weeks after Greb was safely dead, he surfaced again among the middleweights and took the crown.

Mickey: 1, the World: 0

The first time the Toy Bulldog met the "Nebraska Wildcat," Ace Hudkins, was at Chicago's Comiskey Park in the pouring rain. Mickey won the judges' decision. He did not, however, take the crowd's decision, and the more outspoken among them vented their dissent by throwing bottles and shattering the arc lights overhead. Most of the boxing writers scrambling at ringside preferred the skill displayed by the judges' pick even if it was Hudkins who had forced the fight.

Ace Hudkins had been forcing fights from the moment he came out swinging from his mother's womb. He was one of nine siblings from the wrong side of town. We all knew him—he was that kid with ill-fitting clothes and a chip the size of Gibraltar on his shoulder.

When a reporter from the *Los Angeles Times* met him at his training camp, he made the astute observation that Hudkins was the kind of man who could "chew iron and spit rust." His pen trembled just a bit when Hudkins snarled at him, "You can put this down right now, I've ruined more fighters than any other guy in the ring today—any other guy in the ring today . . . nobody can lick me . . . Maybe Mickey Walker would like to read that." If Mickey's training camp up in the Ventura Hills was a delivery stop for the *Times*, we can be assured that the sports pages held up in his meaty paws were steady, barring a breeze.

Come fight time, those meaty paws steadily de-clawed the ripping, slashing brawler. Any lingering doubt about Mickey's supremacy was banished for good when he took every round against Hudkins, save one scored even. The bulldog tamed the wildcat, took it for a walk, yanked its tail, booted it until it screeched, and showed it who was boss. He did so less like a bulldog and more like a park ranger who set bait and sprung traps in every round.

Hudkins' relentless, devil-may-care attack was reduced to impotence this time. "Come on and fight! Come on!" Hudkins yelled between left hooks that cut his eye and tore his lip. Mickey staggered Hudkins repeatedly, picking off his strenuous swings with ease and countering to the body and head with short, powerful shots. It was the worst beating Hudkins absorbed in one hundred and three career bouts. After the final bell, Hudkins was a bloody mess as he wobbled over to congratulate his conqueror.

The fans went home to read the evening edition of the *Times*, which was blaring an alarm: "CRASH SEVEREST RECORDED IN MODERN HISTORY . . . BOTTOM DROPS OUT." The date was October 29, 1929—Black Tuesday. The Great Depression had begun.

Feeling blue at the dawn of a new decade? Don't. Eighty years ago it was much worse. Breadlines stretched for blocks as the proud were humbled and the humble were hungry. Speakeasies were full and so were the churches, where mothers lit candles and men in suits sobbed in pews. Radio personality Will Rogers remarked that people had to stand in line to get a window to jump out of and speculators were selling space for bodies at the bottom of the East River. Everything in the country seemed to crash at once.

Ace Hudkins wobbled but did not crash to the canvas the night he faced a peaking Mickey Walker. He crashed later. His boxing career wound down quickly after 1929 and he became a roaring alcoholic. He was sued twice, once for fracturing the skull of a pedestrian and another after his live-in girlfriend accused him of assault. He was arrested no less than ten times for drunk driving and drunken brawls, including one with the police. In 1933, at the height of the Depression, his bank account was shot, and so was he—twice in the chest.

Meanwhile, Mickey, who at the end of the Hudkins rematch sported a pinkish hue on his cheeks from the moderate exercise, would become an artist.

His prudence at Wrigley Field stood in stark contrast to both the feral fighting method of Hudkins and the panic that wrecked Wall Street. He'd need such prudence where he was going. Big purses, like big investments, bring big risks. Sure it's nice to get rich, but one must be careful when dealing with large sums, or large some-ones.

The bulldog got out of the yard and went charging into the land of the giants.

Snapping at the Heels of History

"When I got in the ring and got a look at him," Mickey re-called about Edward Wright, "I nearly fainted before I got out there to throw a punch." Wright was no little wildcat like Hudkins. His nickname was "Bearcat," and he was a big, bad, black heavyweight who stood over six feet tall and reportedly weighed two hundred and fifty pounds. He fought out of Omaha, Nebraska and held wins over faded legends Sam Langford and Jack Johnson. Mickey stood five feet seven inches with his shoes on and weighed about as much as his opponent's suitcase. When they stood facing each other at ring center, Bearcat looked like he could pick him up like a favorite nephew and give him a kiss.

"It was my idea to fight the big guys," Mickey said. "The big guys were slower." In other words, after almost a hundred and twenty-five bouts in twelve years, and just as youth and speed were beginning to fade with age, Mickey began fighting heavyweights as a matter of course—because they were "easier."

Bearcat Wright took offense to that big idea and began his quar-rel with Mickey the way every heavyweight should when little guys have aspirations—he went straight at him. A monstrous shot spilled Mickey onto the canvas like a bucket of paint. But Mickey not only got up, he carried the fight to his opponent from that moment on. Along the way he must have borrowed a ladder because it was Bearcat who went down in the second round.

Mickey had the heavyweight cornered and was still snarling at the last bell.

He trotted fearlessly in his new yard, sometimes so fearlessly he'd forget to be prudent. He'd blow off training, put on his glad rags, and hit the gin mills. On the eve of the Kentucky Derby in 1930, he was scheduled to fight heavyweight Paul Swiderski, but it was called off that afternoon. So off he went, pub crawling with a few boxing writers and "really tied one on." Negotiations went on without him. They ended successfully and the fight was back on, though half the main event wasn't found until eight that evening. No coffee was black enough and no shower cold enough to sober him up before fight time. Half held up by manager Doc Kearns, he lurched down the aisle and crawled into the ring.

The dailies will tell you that Mickey went down several times in round one, but there should be an asterisk attached. Swiderski had less to do with it than the bartenders around Louisville. With thirty seconds left in the round, Mickey was on one knee, and as the count reached nine, the bell clanged. Kearns had muscled the timekeeper out of the way and struck it early. An enraged Swiderski ran over and socked Mickey on the snout. Kearns tried to sock him back and bedlam broke out. "Next thing I knew," he said, "there were a hundred guys in the ring, all of them punching." Dizzy Mickey thought he was in a street fight and started swinging at whomever, and popped Kearns on the jaw. The fighter then had to drag his manager to the corner.

In the next round, Mickey went down again and the armory's lights went out. Many suspected that Kearns did it. "The story that I turned out the lights to save Walker from being knocked out isn't true," Kearns said in 1948. "I didn't turn out the lights. Not that it wouldn't have been a good idea. I didn't turn out the lights because I couldn't find the switch." Those who knew Kearns were sure that he had someone else do it.

After the delay, Mickey sobered up just enough to burp his way to a decision win.

All told, Mickey whipped about sixteen big dogs, "big bums" he called them, including top-ten contenders Johnny Risko and King

Levinsky. The biggest among them was Arthur De Kuh who was six feet three inches and two hundred and twenty-three pounds. The best among them, though far from the most popular, was number-one contender Jack Sharkey.

July 22, 1931, Ebbets Field. Westbrook Pegler watched Mickey stride confidently past press row and into the ring to face the six-foot Sharkey. He shook his head, not only because of Mickey's age and size, but also because of his lifestyle. "During the last four or five years," he wrote in the days before the bout, "Mickey has been a member of the night side, so, for one thing, there isn't enough of him and, for another thing, what there is of him isn't as good as it would have been if he had always gone to bed at 9 p.m."

Pegler was never one to hide his pessimism under a bushel basket. "Naturally," he quipped, "in promoting the prizefight, the shrewd thing to do is keep on suggesting this remote possibility [that Mickey can win] until, by force of reiteration, it becomes a live, tingling hope."

His lucid mind then drifted to horses:

> *Often times, at a horse track, a party will bet more or less money on some poor weary steed at odds of fifty to one or some such figure and, just by wishing alone, will develop a beautiful picture of that horse winning the race by the time they go to the post. Then the horse jumps a few yards and sits down to bat a whisker of hay out of his ear with a hind foot and finishes nowhere at all, but the customer had the fun of hoping, anyway.*

Evidently, Pegler didn't take a trip to New Jersey to watch Mickey train. Now pushing thirty, the ex-champion was better conditioned than he'd been in years.

Three minutes into the match, Pegler raised an eyebrow. By the third round, he and the rest of the scribes sat in silence while their

cynicism melted under the lights. Yesterday, they were laughing behind typewriters and setting astronomical odds against Mickey. Today, they wore invisible dunce caps while twenty-five thousand fans
rooted behind them. The short ones stood on their chairs.

In the seventh round, Pegler watched Mickey come "swinging
in under Sharkey's cautious defensive works with the low roll of a
vaudeville baboon on roller skates" to land a right that sent Sharkey
stumbling backwards to the ropes. Mickey took a right flush on the
chin in the eleventh but shook it off and landed an uppercut that
sent Sharkey to the ropes again on rubber legs. For fifteen rounds, he
treated giants the way little guys should, with a persuasive prescription of overhands and in close where long arms get in the way and
short ones rule the day.

Mickey's style had once been compared to watching major sur-
gery done with an oar by a neophyte who confused aggression with
mindlessness. This performance spoke for itself. Mickey bobbed and
weaved while the soon-to-be heavyweight champion of the world
missed and missed again "—in the manner of a man throwing shoes
out a window at a singing tomcat," wrote Pegler. "Walker blocked
many of these blows, squatted under many others," he added, "and
soaked up some with a curious rolling away motion which eased the
impact." As the bells tolled and the rounds waned, Sharkey grew
desperate.

He landed low blows. Mickey ignored them.

He put his hands up to protect his face. Mickey switched the
attack to the body.

He stood straighter or leaned back to draw on his height advantage. Mickey *jumped*.

Sharkey, known for a level of skill rare in his weight class, was
facing a superior ring general who would explode the myth that bigger means better.

After the bout, the humbled heavyweight was unusually gracious. This man, he said, "is a great little fighter and don't let anyone tell you he can't hurt." Mickey was still chomping at the bit.

"I could fight fifteen more like it right now," he said as his eyes twinkled over a contagious smile. "I thought I won all right, but that don't matter." The official result of the bout was a draw, but it was Mickey who gave Sharkey a "pretty thorough licking" out-scoring him "by the difference between fifteen dollars and fifteen cents," said the scribe who compared him to a weary steed only the week before.

Pegler may not have realized it yet, but he had just witnessed one of boxing history's greatest performances, and the assumption here is that he promptly became an enthusiastic convert to the cause of short people, fighting Irish, and long odds.

The next afternoon he was almost certainly spotted ten miles west, jumping up and down at Jamaica Racetrack, where he lost his shirt.

MICKEY WALKER'S SCORECARD

—25 points—
Quality of Opposition: 24.4

—15 points—
Ring Generalship: 14.4
Longevity: 14.6
Dominance: 14.5

—10 points—
Durability: 8.6
P/LO: 10
Intangibles: 9.7

Total *96.2*

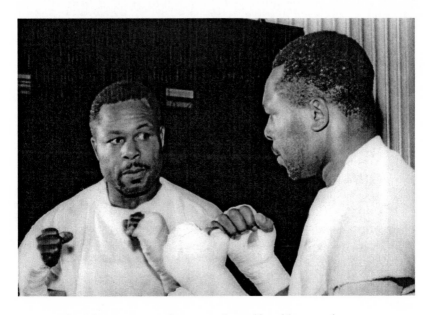

The Ole Mongoose reflects upon himself and his grand mission.
(Rogers Photo Archive)

The Sixth God of War

Time is a strange brew.
—Archie Moore

Archie Moore may have needed smelling salts after they told him he was finally getting a crack at Joey Maxim's light heavyweight crown. It was the Yuletide season of 1952, and the "Ole Mongoose" was thirty-six years old with more than one hundred and sixty professional bouts behind him. He could have used a handrail to climb the ringside stairs.

Moore was aging all right, but he was an aging puncher, and that meant something. Remember your grandfather's vice-grip of a handshake? Men get stronger as they age. With legs getting rigid with mileage, Moore found it easier to plant his feet and punch like hell.

He was always a powerful fighter and, partially because of that, an avoided fighter. He had been ranked as a middleweight from 1940 through 1944 and ranked as a light heavyweight for the next eight years. Two of his most dangerous opponents were retired by the time he fought Maxim, Charley Burley in 1950 and Eddie Booker in 1944. Neither of them was able to get a world title shot and all three had to take jobs outside of boxing at one time or another: Burley at an aircraft plant, Booker as a red cap porter, and Moore as a night watchman. "I am often asked why, when both Burley and Booker beat me, neither one got to the top, whereas I did," the introspective Moore said. "Well, I guess it's the way I sized things up. I felt I had two opponents—other boxers and Father Time." Discouragement, he said, "can KO a boxer even before he has a chance to step into the ring."

Moore may have had a main event against Father Time, but he never forgot the preliminary brawls early in his career. After a three-month, seven-fight jaunt in Australia in 1940, he dropped anchor in California at the age of twenty-three and joined the ranks of other great black boxers then campaigning on the west coast. Moore and the set remembered as Murderers' Row fought among themselves like lions for peanuts not far enough from the San Diego Zoo. All told, Moore, Burley, Booker, Jack Chase, Lloyd Marshall, Little Tiger Wade, Bert Lytell, Holman Williams, and Cocoa Kid fought each other eighty times. Moore's record against them was 10-5-3 with four knockouts, which was about as good as it got.

Those internecine wars furnished all of them with a wealth of experience, though their purses weren't even big enough to furnish a house. And they opened no doors.

A frustrated Burley hung up the gloves and took a job as a garbage man for the city of Pittsburgh. Wade was in and out of retirement throughout his career because no one wanted to fight him. Booker was forced out after an eye injury got progressively worse. Lytell was blackballed when he was just twenty-seven years old and was reduced to sparring for a flat rate against world middleweight champion Randy Turpin. Chase, Marshall, Williams, and Cocoa Kid were chewed up and spat out of the ring by their mid-thirties. Bitterness was a contagion for ignored fighters like the Mongoose and Murderers' Row.

Perhaps Moore's greatest triumph, then, was a spiritual one.

He had ulcers that ruptured the day after a brutal bout with Booker and landed him in the hospital for thirty-eight days. He was close to death. After self-diagnosing the true causes of his ailment, he picked up a mirror and saw a face etched with tension. It was the face of millions of African American men seething under the surface, held down by invisible chains. Moore found himself holding onto negative feelings, and it had done a number not only on his health but also on his character. So he wrote his own prescription for healing remedies that predated the New Age movement by three decades—he listened to jazz, learned to take therapeutic naps, mastered his pseudo-scientific theories of "breathology," "escapism," and "relaxism," and overcame what ailed him.

It was an achievement that stands as a monument to inspire us all. Moore went deep into an internal cave and battled the dragons lurking in his own humanity. What emerged was a philosopher-king who took hold of a grand mission and slung it on his back. He would not only honor an old promise made to his aunt to refrain from drinking, smoking, or "doing anything shameful in the ring," he also made a new one to himself. Long before Bernard Hopkins was even born, he ignored time and its creaking warnings, and forced his way through the gates of a kingdom that was rightfully his.

"I know I can beat Maxim," he told reporters. "I always did believe I could beat him."

A.J. Liebling agreed. Moore reminded him of "a supreme exponent of *bel canto* who sees himself crowded out of the opera house by a guy who can only shout." The perennial top contender took matters into his own hands and began writing letters to sports editors all over the country. "I pleaded, I cursed," he said. "I demanded a shot at Maxim's crown." Joey Maxim's manager was the go-to man, and it just so happened that Maxim's manager was Doc Kearns, the same Doc Kearns who once managed Mickey Walker. By then, Kearns had snow on the roof. His greediness was, by contrast, evergreen, and he finally yielded, but only after he received a guaranteed purse of $100,000 for Maxim. Moore signed despite the fact that his end would be a paltry $800.

Most fight fans knew what was what and who was who and the odds reflected that. They were set at twelve-to-five against the champion. Losing was unthinkable for a challenger who remembered well the trials of Charley Burley. "I've been waiting a long time," Moore said with quiet intensity. "I've got to win."

He had another reason to win, another motivation that fluttered deep inside of him: he had made arrangements for his divorced parents to sit ringside at the arena in St. Louis. A man who banishes bitterness from his heart does funny things, and this man forgave his parents for sending him away to his aunt and uncle when he was barely a year old. "I just wanted my father and my mother to see me win the title, together," he told *Sports Illustrated* in 1989. "I wanted to look down on them, next to each other, at that moment. And I did."

Moore then turned his attention to the king on his throne, on *his* throne.

The bell that began the main event was momentous. In a few minutes it became clear that it was ringing for him and tolling for Maxim. A right hand dented Maxim's square jaw in the first round and he forced a clinch. Maxim, born Giuseppe Antonio Berardinelli, had a repeating left jab that recalled a Maxim machine gun, thus the name. As Moore applied his hardware and demonstrated superior technical know-how, Maxim's own considerable skills were neutralized and his jab shot blanks. The champion was hurt in every round after the seventh. "Time and again," reported the Associated Press, "Moore unleashed the full fury of almost a decade of frustration as the 'uncrowned champion.'"

Kearns may have finagled a $100,000 retirement fund for the inevitable dethronement of his boy, but some of those funds had to be earmarked for medical bills. Maxim was gashed and swollen when his crown fell off.

Moore caught that crown with nimble hands.

At the end of fifteen rounds, Moore's manager attempted to lift him in the air to celebrate, but he would have none of it. "Just slip my robe on my shoulders," the new old king ordered. "There's nothing to get excited about. I could've won this thing twelve years ago if I'd had the chance."

Only minutes after his victory, Moore announced his intentions. "I'm going to put some life in the division. Any contender who deserves a chance will get it." And the old Mongoose was every bit as good as his word. His predecessors' sins of avoidance were spotlighted by a champion who faced all-comers—including Maxim, twice.

With this remarkable victory, Moore was escorted out of what he called the murky twilight and into the radiance of worldwide celebrity. It was long overdue. The charismatic light heavyweight king was interviewed often and would not allow the public to forget the names of those fierce and forgotten men he faced in his youth. He would tip his crown to them and his humanity shined when he did.

It is poignant when you think about it. But for his longevity and single-mindedness, the name "Archie Moore" would surely have been added by history to the ranks of Murderers' Row—as another great coulda' been. Instead, he became the unlikeliest of destiny's children, an old man spanking contenders for the sheer fun of it.

Late wars followed his ascension to the purple, including a dramatic one against Yvon Durelle and memorable campaigns in the heavyweight division against Rocky Marciano and Muhammad Ali. Indeed, the names on Moore's resume read like graffiti at the Roman Pantheon. One of those names was Jimmy Bivins whom he had beaten three times. When asked who was the greatest of the eight world champions he faced, Bivins told THE RING, "The one guy who stands out—and he stands out in everyone's mind—is Archie Moore. I thought he was the greatest fighter in the world. He could punch and he could box. But he could really punch. He wasn't afraid of nobody."

He came out of an era when men fought more often for less money and working conditions were considerably rougher than they are today. He managed to defeat world-class middleweights, light heavyweights, and heavyweights, though he was essentially a middleweight with a paunch. He overcame seven Hall of Famers. The record should read eight; a prime Willie Pastrano escaped with a hotly disputed draw after Moore chased him around the ring on forty-five-year-old legs. That was in 1962. Moore had his first professional fight in 1935.

Many civilians cannot understand why anyone would choose Moore's profession for a living, and even fighters themselves would be hard-pressed to explain how a man could fight two hundred and twenty times over twenty-eight years. Placing one's health and well-being at such risk so often for so long seems to be utter folly, if not madness. Moore was an exception that proved the rule. He was the antique that outperformed newer models, a well-mannered eccentric who would show up at weigh-ins resplendent in a top hat and tuxedo, twirling a walking stick. At times he'd step onto the scale buck naked. And even had he been a bit mad, there was a touch of genius in it—his showmanship complemented the staggering skillfulness of his craft and boosted box-office receipts.

In the end, Archie Moore's motivation was neither madness nor money.

It was love.

"Boxing is magnificent," he told a journalist late in life, his eyes softening with affection. "It's beautiful to know. Oh, the price can be very dear. You've got to marry it. And so I did. Boxing was my lover. It was my lady."

ARCHIE MOORE'S SCORECARD

—25 points—
Quality of Opposition: 24.7

—15 points—
Ring Generalship: 14.6
Longevity: 15
Dominance: 14.8

—10 points—
Durability: 8
P/LO: 9.6
Intangibles: 9.7

Total *96.4*

The Hands of Stone (right) and his greatest nemesis, Sugar Ray Leonard. (Rogers Photo Achive)

The Fifth God of War

Yield to the god.
—Aeneid, bk. V, 1. 467

A battered and bloodied world welterweight champion glowered at his corner men as the thirteenth round was about to begin. "If you stop this fight," he said, "I'll never talk to you the rest of my life." In the opposite corner, a surging Henry Armstrong sprang out of his corner at the bell. Trainer Ray Arcel, a cotton swab in his mouth, watched the last three rounds with Barney Ross's words echoing in his ears and a prayer on his lips. He prayed not that Ross would win, but that he would survive.

The vanquished champion was brought back to the hotel where Arcel put hot towels on his swollen face and tended to his wounds. He stayed with him four days and four nights.

That was 1938. Arcel had already been in the fight game two decades. He was at Stillman's Gym from the beginning and taught hundreds of young men how to fight over a seven-decade career.

Arcel met Freddie Brown at Stillman's. Brown grew up on Forsythe Street in the Lower East Side not three miles from Benny Leonard's house. He began training in the 1920s and had what A.J. Liebling described as the unmistakable appearance of old fighters: "small men with mashed noses and quick eyes" and a chewed-up stogie stuck on his lip that contrasted nicely with the clean cotton swab of Arcel.

Mangos

Twenty-year-old Roberto Duran's American debut was at Madison Square Garden. Thirteen thousand, two hundred and eleven ticket-buyers watched him lay out Benny Huertas like a red carpet in less than a minute. Dave Anderson covered the fight for the *New York Times*. "Remember the name," he advised.

Arcel was just sitting down when that stone fist crashed on Huertas' temple. As the Panamanian left the ring on his way to the dressing room, he startled the old man again when he kissed him on the cheek. A month later Duran would be introduced to Brown and the triumvirate would be complete.

"When I came into his camp in 1972, he was just a slugger until I taught him finesse," Brown remembered. A slugger? Duran was worse than that. He was a savage, a Roman wolf-child placed in a civilizing school where ancient masters taught the art of war. Agrippina summoned Seneca to tutor a young Nero. Duran's manager summoned Arcel. Arcel brought in Brown. It took not one, but two eminent teachers to tame Duran, and Brown bore the brunt of it—camping outside of his door to chase away the broads, dragging him out of bed at dawn for roadwork, locking up the pantry.

The two old men never did completely civilize their pupil, though they did better than Seneca—Nero used Christians as torches to light the streets of Rome. Duran listened, and because he listened, he lit up fighters in six weight classes.

In 1972, Duran indecently assaulted lightweight champion Ken Buchanan and snatched his crown. His reign of terror lasted six years and twelve defenses.

"The only guy we had like him," Brown told Pete Hamill, "is Henry Armstrong." Brown and Arcel knew the combined value of explosiveness and intelligence in the ring. "Boxing is brain over brawn," said Arcel whenever the subject came up. "If you can't think, you're just another bum in the park." Duran was not only "one of the most vicious fighters we've ever had," added Brown, "[he was] one of the smartest."

Duran was destined to invade the welterweight division. When he did, it was as deep as it ever was. Waiting for him were two bangers in Pipino Cuevas and Thomas Hearns, defensive specialist Wilfred Benitez, boxer Carlos Palomino, and the smiling celebrity who lorded over them all—the boxer-puncher Ray Leonard.

Malice

By the end of 1979, a clash between Leonard and Duran was almost certain. Duran had already retired former welterweight champion Palomino in a dominant performance, while Leonard stopped Benitez and took the title. They fought separately on the Larry Holmes-Earnie Shavers undercard and Leonard's trainer Angelo Dundee watched the Duran bout very carefully. "Duran is thought of as a rough guy, but he's not rough," he observed. "He's smart and slick."

Arcel, eighty-one, and Brown, seventy-three, were watching Leonard as well, though they were very familiar with his style and how to beat it. They had already trained about thirty world champions between them. Fifty-eight-year-old Dundee had trained nine. In fact, Dundee's novitiate was at Stillman's Gym where he handed towels to the two masters he now matched wits with.

The posturing began soon enough. At Gleason's Gym, Leonard was watching Duran skip rope when Duran spotted him and began lashing the rope with uncanny speed—while squatting. At a press conference at the Waldorf-Astoria Hotel in New York City, Duran cuffed Leonard. Two days before the fight, both men were at an indoor mall in Montreal, and Duran learned just enough English to yell, "Two more days! Two more days!" Leonard blew a kiss, and Duran charged at him and had to be restrained.

Duran was getting mean, but it was Leonard who had every physical advantage. He was younger, faster, taller, and bigger. "I'm not Ali," Leonard insisted to the pundits. "Sure, maybe at the start I was trying to do his shuffle or his rope-a-dope, but not now."

Duran looked pudgy in his last two outings, and the previous three welterweights he faced went the full ten rounds. Never before had three in a row gone the distance with him, and there was chatter about not only his power at welterweight but also his motivation. Duran himself admitted that he was not always committed to training and his trainers did too, though a warning was attached: "When you're fighting smear cases and you're the best fighter around, it's hard to be interested, but now he's inspired, and when he's inspired, he's relentless," Arcel said. "Leonard can't beat this guy."

The odds makers disagreed. Duran was a nine-to-five underdog.

Leonard was confident enough to ask permission from an aging Ray Robinson to borrow "Sugar," but he couldn't have anticipated how many lumps he'd get from Duran, who had more in common with fighters from Robinson's era than he ever would.

As Leonard made his way toward the ring on June 20, 1980, Duran shadow boxed his own demons in the red corner. Both were in the best condition of their lives, though Duran exuded something like preternatural malevolence. Arcel had already promised that we would witness "the darndest fight" we ever saw—and we did.

Duran had promised to use "old tricks" against Leonard. *Old tricks.* Freddie Brown's fingerprints were all over the place. He trained him at Grossinger's Resort in the Catskills, where he worked with Rocky Marciano in the 1950s and Joey Archer in the 1960s. Brown had more tricks than a cathouse. Duran could be seen holding Leonard in the crook of his arms to stop incoming shots and create the perception that Leonard was doing nothing. Then there was the "Fitzsimmons shift." Dundee himself might never have heard of it, but he saw it all right: ". . . if [Duran] missed you with an overhand right," he observed, "he'd turn southpaw and come back with a left hook to the body." Duran executed it against Leonard in the fifth, seventh, and eighth rounds. Bob Fitzsimmons invented it and used it to implode Gentleman Jim Corbett in 1897. It's a peach of a move.

Stone Hands controlled the action in this career-defining bout, and his savvy was no less a deciding factor than his savagery. But make no mistake; the Sugar Man pushed him almost beyond his limits. And there were over forty-six thousand witnesses. Every now and then, one of them, a thin and solitary Nicaraguan with a mustache could be seen standing up from his seat and waving a little Panamanian flag. It was Alexis Arguello.

Myths
Duran's strategy was drilled into him. He was instructed to be elusive against the jab, close the distance, crowd Leonard, and hammer the body.

Leonard's aggressive strategy made things more, not less, difficult to cope with for precisely the reason that Dundee had alluded to: good little guys don't beat good big guys. "In this fight, Duran's not the puncher," he said. "My guy is." The respective knockout percentages over their previous five fights confirm this; Duran's was forty percent, Leonard's one hundred.

Leonard promised to stand and fight more than expected. "They all think I'm going to run. I'm not," he said to *New York* magazine. "I'm not changing my style at all . . . he'll be beaten to the punch . . . those are the facts," he continued. "What's going to beat Roberto Duran is Sugar Ray Leonard."

Dundee substantiated this in his autobiography. His strategy became certain from the moment that he watched the films and deconstructed Duran's style. Dundee said that Duran was a "heel-to-toe guy. He takes two steps to get to you. So the idea was not to give him those two steps, not to move too far away because the more distance you gave him, the more effective he was. What you can't do in the face of Duran's aggression was run from it, because then he picks up momentum. My guy wasn't going to run from him."

So there you have it.

Leonard's strategy in Montreal was deliberate and sound. After it failed, Dundee and Leonard revised history and a willing press has gone along with it ever since. We've been spoon-fed a fable that has long-since crystallized into orthodox boxing lore. It is the archetypal image of the Latin bully who "tricked" our all-American hero into an alley fight, and it sprang from the idea that Leonard "did not fight his fight" because Duran challenged his masculinity.

The problem is that the idea is at complete odds with Leonard and Dundee's statements about Leonard's clear physical advantages and the strategy that would be formed around those advantages. It contradicts Dundee's earlier statements about Duran's high level of skill, and it contradicts statements both had made immediately after the bout—before they had time to think about posterity: "You've got to give credit to Duran," Dundee told journalists. "He makes you fight his fight." When asked why he fought Duran's fight, Leonard said he had "no alternative."

Since then, Leonard's loss to Duran has been cleverly spun, repackaged, and sold at a reduced price. It's time to find our receipt and exchange a fable for the facts. And the facts begin with this: when both fighters were at their best, Duran was better.

Memento Mori

Duran's record stood at 72-1 with fifty-six knockouts. As he simmered down in the aftermath of the fight, the magnitude of it all set in. He knew that Leonard was great. At the post-fight press conference, he was asked if Leonard was the toughest opponent he ever faced. Duran, his face scuffed and swollen, thought for a moment. "Si," he said, ". . . si."

And then something changed. Whatever it was that raged inside Roberto Duran—a legion of devils, his hatred of Leonard, the memory of a child begging on the streets of Chorrillo—faded from that moment. He became more sedate. After thirteen years of *pasion violenta* and after a victory that is almost without equal in the annals of boxing history, he fell like all who forget that they are mortal, and his humiliation would be so complete that it would obscure everything else.

Old embers would flare up only sporadically after the fateful year of 1980. Three times more he would remind the world of his greatness against men that no natural lightweight in his right mind would challenge. By then the two old men had walked away. Arcel and Brown joined us in the audience and watched a melting legend fight youngsters. As the curtain slowly descended on a career that would span five decades, there was little left that recalled what he was; just some old tricks in an arsenal ransacked by age and an unbecoming appetite.

But what he was should not be eclipsed. It should be remembered: When the splendor that was Sugar Ray Leonard entranced America, Brown and Arcel closed the blinds and applied old school methods in the shadow of Stillman's Gym. They brought a Panamanian to a peak of human performance so perfect in its blend of science and ferocity that it would never be approached again—by Duran or anyone else.

Fifteen rounds unveiled a god of war.

After the final bell, a jubilant Duran leaps into the air. Before he lands he sees Leonard daring to raise his arms in victory and the coals of his eyes burn. He shoves and spits at his adversary, then stalks toward the ropes at ringside and grabs his crotch as he hurls Spanish epithets. Arcel tries to calm him down. The announcer shouts "le nouveau!" into the microphone, and victorious, the raging champion is hoisted up above the crowd—above the world—still cursing the vanquished.

This is Duran.

ROBERTO DURAN'S SCORECARD

—25 points—
Quality of Opposition: 24.1

—15 points—
Ring Generalship: 14.7
Longevity: 14.8
Dominance: 14.9

—10 points—
Durability: 9.8
P/LO: 9.7
Intangibles: 8.5

Total *96.5*

*Ezzard Charles with wife Gladys in 1970,
nearing the end and still smiling.*
(Historic Images)

The Fourth God of War

He has shown you, o man, what is good.
And what does the Lord require of you?
To act justly, to love mercy, and to walk humbly with your God.
—Micah 6:8

Lou Ambers landed a shot to the jaw, and when Tony Scarpati went down, his head bounced off the canvas. He died three days later. "Every once in a while," Ambers remembered, "I'd look in that corner and I'd see like a picture of Tony, God rest his soul."

Sugar Ray Robinson had a grim premonition before facing Jimmy Doyle and regretted going through with that bout. "I was busted up," Robinson said after Doyle died, "and for a long time after that I could fight just hard enough to win."

Twenty-year-old Sam Baroudi had another kind of premonition. In the summer of 1947, he knocked out Glenn Newton Smith. Smith collapsed in the dressing room and succumbed to a cerebral hemorrhage. Six months later Baroudi fought light heavyweight Ezzard Charles. Baroudi had never been stopped in any of his fifty-two previous bouts. He was fighting out of a crouch in the tenth round when Ezzard landed three hard shots to the head, which caused his eyes to glaze. A left to the body sent him down. He was carried out of Chicago Stadium on a stretcher and died five hours later.

The day after the fight, a middle-aged man arrived in Chicago from Akron, Ohio to claim the body. It was Baroudi's father. "This was a terrible accident," he told Ezzard. "Our family bears no bitterness at all towards you. Don't give up on your career." A charity match was set up at Ezzard's request and a certified check of $15,880 was given to the Baroudi family. Ezzard donated his entire purse.

Reluctantly, the number-one light heavyweight contender continued with his career, but he would never again compete in his natural division. He'd only fight heavyweights, as if afraid of injuring men his own size. A.J. Liebling got the impression that Ezzard suffered from emotional blocks in the heat of battle and saw in him an "intuitive aversion to violence" that would "set in like ice on a pond." Once feared for his "black-out" punches, his clean knockout rate of forty-four percent before the Baroudi fight dropped to twenty-eight percent after it. His popularity dropped with it.

Ghosts, guilt, and the evaporation of the "killer instinct" are common symptoms for boxers whose hands kill an opponent. For Ezzard the symptoms were severe.

He was named after Dr. Webster Pierce Ezzard, the obstetrician who delivered him in 1921, and was raised by his grandmother Maude Foster and a great grandmother named Belle Russell who was born a slave. They taught him to pray, to read the Bible every day, and to place no value on human applause.

Ezzard had a smile that was radiant enough to fill a room, but he wasn't raised to be charismatic. As the press found out soon enough, a conversation with him could be about as mutual as brushing your teeth. He wasn't raised to avoid a challenge either, and he didn't, though others failed to extend him the same courtesy. He was ducked for years by the same light heavyweight champions who ducked Archie Moore, despite the fact that he cleaned out the field of contenders—including Archie Moore.

His prime ended with no laurels and no belts. It ended with Sam Baroudi's last breaths.

Ezzard is most remembered for the unexpected stands he made late in his career against Rocky Marciano. He fought hammer and tong, even giving up reading his books because they had become "a distraction." "Rough and crude," he told Budd Schulberg. "I gotta be rough and crude." After the first fight, photographs of his face were presented in eighteen different degrees of contortion at the end of Marciano's fists in LIFE magazine. "This Is What Charles Took" proclaimed the title.

By 1955, symptoms of amyotrophic lateral sclerosis (ALS) were becoming evident. "Looking back now," recalled Ray Arcel, "it's easy to see that Ezzard was in the early stages of the illness that eventually killed him. But at the time I just thought he was getting older. He wasn't able to do the things he'd always done. He'd get tired. His coordination wasn't there." It affected his legs first, which explains why this once versatile technician struggled against stumblebums as his career waned. By then the crowds were booing him.

Sportswriters picked up on his childhood nickname of "Snooky" and started calling him "Snooks," but with disdain, not affection. Television audiences missed the best years of his career. Most never saw what he was before the face of Sam Baroudi looked at him behind every opponent's guard; what he was before his body began to betray him. They saw only an aging fighter struggling to hold on to his dignity and perhaps win more than he lost. That image has persevered for decades.

That image is a false one and should be undone. At his best, this unpretentious man was one of history's supreme boxer-punchers. In his capable hands, the manly art of self-defense was baptized by fire into something godly.

This is his transfiguration.

Inheriting the Earth

In the beginning, sportswriters called him the "Cincinnati School Boy," but with affection, not disdain. With a fledgling record of 17-1, he faced Hall of Famer Teddy Yarosz. Yarosz's record was 106-16-3. The fact that the clever Yarosz had beaten a parade of dangerous fighters made no difference. Ray Arcel himself was in his corner but that made no difference either. Yarosz only landed a handful of lefts and Ezzard cruised to a decision win.

In January 1942, Ezzard fought top contender Anton Christo-
foridis (35-10-6) and handed him his first stoppage loss, shocking
everyone except for those in Cincinnati who already knew how great
he was. In March, he fought to a draw with a former middleweight
champion, Ken Overlin (130-19-7). Overlin took a split decision
over him the previous year—when Ezzard was a junior at Woodward
High School.

His principal remembered seeing him arrive for classes with a
shiner or two the morning after a fight. It impressed him how Ezzard
was almost always on time despite his moonlighting.

In May, when he fought the feared and avoided Charley Burley
(51-5) in Pittsburgh, he had to short-change training to cram for his
final examinations.

Burley was installed as a ten-to-eight favorite.

Ezzard outpunched him.

Even as New York City buzzed about Burley's shocking defeat and
the name of his conqueror was spoken with reverence at Stillman's
Gym, Ezzard was hurrying back home to Cincinnati in time to grad-
uate with his class. He also got his car keys back. His grandmother
had taken them away for two weeks after the conqueror missed his
curfew. With grandma smiling again, the proud high school gradu-
ate hopped a train back to Pennsylvania to prove that the win over
Burley was no fluke.

The return bout was even money.

Ezzard outboxed him.

No man alive had defeated Burley twice in a row. Ezzard did it
with a combination of power shots off the front foot and sheer ability off the back foot. Even Arcel was in awe. Those two victories, he
said, were "the first time I realized Charles was a great boxer." His
next four victories were almost as impressive and launched him into
serious contention for both the middleweight and light heavyweight
crowns. Four straight knockouts of serious fighters (three of whom
were never counted out in a combined total of ninety-two fights)
were tough to ignore.

It was the summer of '42, and Ezzard Charles had come of age. Managers were hiding under their hats. It took fellow-great Jimmy Bivins to alleviate anxieties with a decision win, and then Lloyd Marshall cooled Ezzard off with an eighth round stoppage.

Within two years the "School Boy" would evolve into "The Cincinnati Cobra" and strike through his natural habitat like no one ever had before or ever will again. Atop the heap of casualties was a mongoose: Archie Moore could neither outslug nor outwit this cobra despite three desperate tries. Ezzard also avenged his loss to Bivins four times and knocked Marshall out twice.

During a ten-year span, he faced down a platoon of ring generals in three divisions eighteen times and then dethroned an idol whose color photograph was tacked to his bedroom wall.

That idol was Joe Louis.

Arcel was Ezzard's trainer. It was not the first time Arcel had been in the opposite corner from Louis. During the referee's instruction for one of them, Louis took one look at him and said, "You heah again?" After Buddy Baer was knocked flat in one round, Arcel quipped, "Of course I was in shape. I never underestimate Joe Louis. I was ready to pick up whatever came my way." The press called him the "Meat Wagon." Ezzard's victory over Louis was a victory of sorts for the long-suffering trainer, though he didn't see it that way. At the final bell, Arcel came out and embraced both fighters.

The newspapers were forced to finally acknowledge something insiders always knew: that Ezzard was a "much better fighter than the world had thought he was." And that wasn't all. Ezzard became universally accepted as world heavyweight champion. It was September 27, 1950.

Sixty-five-year-old Maude Foster's phone rang that night. On the other end was Ezzard:

"Grandma, I won it for you and the Lord."

"God made you a champion," she said, "and don't forget to thank Him out loud."

He didn't forget.

Days of Grace

When his undiagnosed debilitation began to cripple him a few years later, Ezzard's win-loss ratio tilted sharply for the worse. His last professional bout was in the summer of 1959—the very summer that Lou Stillman sold off his gym on Eighth Avenue.

Citizen Ezzard's decline only continued. Within two years he had no job, no telephone, and a house that was about to be foreclosed. His garage was empty after he sold his cars to buy food for his family. He managed to get a job working with disadvantaged youth for Mayor Daley's Youth Foundation in Chicago, but after 1967, he couldn't walk the block from his house to get there anymore. His legs had stiffened.

The worst was yet to come. Amyotrophic lateral sclerosis affects the brain's ability to send messages to muscles, including those used for respiration. Half of ALS patients die within eighteen months of diagnosis. There is no known cure.

"Oh, it's tough all right," Ezzard said as his health trials began, "not being able to walk like I used to or talk so well. It's a feeling you sort of have, of being all by yourself. That no one can help you."

Ironies abounded. His doctors told him that boxing might have actually benefitted him by delaying the progression of a disease that had begun to develop in his childhood. Long after his days of war, Ezzard found himself doing sit-ups and struggling again with the existential loneliness of a man who fights alone. Only now the sit-ups were an agonizing part of physical therapy and the garish lights of the arena were turned off.

A police officer and friend named John McManus turned those lights back on. With the help of Joe Kellman and Ben Bentley, he organized an event to raise money and defray the mounting medical bills of the ex-champion. "The Ezzard Charles Appreciation Night" was held on November 13, 1968, in the Grand Ballroom of Chicago's Sherman Hotel. For fifteen dollars guests were treated to a sit-down dinner and fight films that they themselves could request through the *Chicago Daily Tribune*.

Many bent noses were in the crowd of thirteen hundred—several of them bent by the guest of honor. Rocky Marciano, whose nose he split into a canyon, was a featured speaker. "I never met a man like Ez in my life," Marciano said as he turned and looked into the eyes of his old foe. "Ez, you fought me about the very best of anybody. I couldn't put you down, and I don't believe anybody can put you down. You've got more spirit than any man I ever knew."

The benefit would raise about $15,000 for Ezzard. It was nearly the exact amount that Ezzard raised for the Baroudi family twenty years earlier. Boxing made a triumphant return into Ezzard's life and like a good corner man in a tough fight; it gave him a lift off the stool. His stool was a wheelchair now. As he struggled to stand up at the podium, Marciano and Archie Moore rushed to his side and lifted him to his feet.

"This is the greatest thing that's ever happened to me," he whispered. "I just want to say . . .thank you. Thank you ..."

Eventually the disease silenced him. Then it paralyzed him.

He lay on his back for a year and three months in a Veteran's Administration hospital as his body wasted away. He had his memories—grand memories that only former fighters are privileged to have, other memories that only the cursed among them must endure. Less than a mile north was Chicago Stadium, where the image of Sam Baroudi collapsed again and again.

As leaves fell to the ground outside the hospital window during the last autumn of his life, the man whose photograph once hung on his wall appeared at the door of room B-804. Joe Louis stood there for a moment and then walked over to the bed. "I could lick you now, champ," he said gently. ". . . I could lick you now."

Ezzard Charles smiled. The radiance of it filled the room.

EZZARD CHARLES'S SCORECARD

—25 points—
Quality of Opposition: 24.6

—15 points—
Ring Generalship: 15·
Longevity: 14.5
Dominance: 14.9

—10 points—
Durability: 8
P/LO: 10
Intangibles: 9.8

Total *96.8*

Hurricane Henry, 1937.
(Photographer: Carl Van Vechten)

The Third God of War

Batten down the hatches!
—*Chambers Journal,* 1883

Henry Armstrong's grandmother was a slave in Mississippi. She was owned by his Irish grandfather whose eyes twinkled at the sight of her. Their son grew up and married a woman who was half-Cherokee. Her name was "America." The couple had fifteen children; the eleventh, Henry, inherited his father's short stature and his mother's strength and work ethic.

The family moved to St. Louis when Henry was still a small child. At sixteen years old, he put on his father's cap and overalls, walked down to the Missouri-Pacific Railroad, and got a job driving spikes with a sledgehammer like John Henry. One day a gust of wind carried a discarded newspaper to his feet. The headline spoke to him: "KID CHOCOLATE EARNS $75,000 FOR HALF HOUR'S WORK." Henry quit his job and ran home to tell his grandmother that he was fixing to be a champion. She looked him up and down and said, "You ain't no Jack Johnson!"

And she was right. The kid with the baggy overalls and a hammer in his hand would become something else, something greater than Jack Johnson.

Henry Armstrong would become a force of nature in the boxing ring. Like those boll weevils that came up and under his family's crops back on the plantation, he'd come up and under his opponent's guard and do to ribs what those critters did to crops. Like the

Tombigbee River that overran its banks and killed their cattle, he'd flood his opponent.

Press row would watch his relentless attack and compare it to a hurricane.

It began as a tempest in a teapot in 1931, when the underfed teenager lost three out of his first four professional fights. Over the next five years, he fought seven draws and suffered eight more setbacks, but stronger frames were getting knocked over. Quite suddenly his elements converged and the forecast turned severe for anyone in his path. Between January 1937 and October 1940, Armstrong posted fifty-nine wins, one heavily disputed loss, one heavily disputed draw, and fifty-one knockouts. In only three years and ten months, Armstrong fought sixty-one times—exactly how many fights Muhammad Ali had over the length of his career—and they weren't scale versions of "bums of the month" either; six Hall of Famers and eight world champions were sent spinning sideways in the ring.

Armstrong reached peak intensity the same year that one of the most powerful natural events in recorded history slammed into the east coast of the United States. The Great Hurricane of 1938 made landfall on September 21 and cut a swath through Long Island, New York, and New England. Only a junior forecaster saw it coming, but his frantic relay was slapped down by his superiors at the U.S. Weather Bureau who expected the storm system to continue on a seaward path. There was no notice, and as a result, no preparation. It hit Long Island at a record speed and changed the landscape of the south coast forever. Over the next three days, the Blue Hills Conservatory in Massachusetts measured peak gusts at one hundred eighty-six miles per hour, and fifty foot waves crashed into the Gloucester shoreline. By the time it was over, seven hundred people had died, sixty-three thousand were left homeless, and two billion trees were uprooted.

"Hurricane Henry" cut another kind of swath through three weight divisions. His managers, the famous Al Jolson, film noir actor George Raft, and Eddie Mead, came up with an idea to pilot him toward three crowns. In an era when boxing recognized only eight kings, toppling three of them would be an unparalleled feat, if he could do it.

That is what it would take, they told Henry, to compete with Joe Louis in a depressed market.

"It sounds pretty good to me," he replied.

The World Featherweight Title (October 29, 1937)

Petey Sarron had been a professional for a dozen years "and looks it," wrote Paul Mickelson. "His eyes are cut, his ears are hard and flat, and he's broken his left hand three times, his right once." He also happened to be champion of the world and in his prime at twenty-nine.

Madison Square Garden's 1937-1938 boxing season opened with Sarron matched up against Armstrong for the featherweight crown. Sarron trained at Pioneer's Gym in Manhattan while Armstrong trained at Stillman's, which may partly explain the two and a half-to-one odds favoring the challenger—that, or the fact that he was on a fifteen fight knockout streak. "This talk don't scare me," Sarron said. "I'm used to it. I found out in America, Africa, and Europe that nobody can beat me at a hundred and twenty-six pounds." Sarron was confident that Armstrong would fade. He reminded all and sundry that while he himself had gone fifteen rounds fifteen times, the challenger never had. "Armstrong isn't fighting a punk this time," he said.

Those who figured that the veteran would let youthful *joie de vivre* sap itself and then take over figured wrong. In the first round, he waded boldly in to meet Armstrong on his own terms and managed to outland him with left hooks. He won the next few rounds as well by inviting Armstrong to open up and countering him. Armstrong made the mistake of trying too hard against a man who knew too much. He got stars in his eyes, went for a spectacular knockout, and got stars in his eyes. His wound-up shots breezed by the moving target, though when they did connect, they hurt. Before long,

Sarron's ribs began rattling like wind chimes under the blustering body attack, and by the fifth round his shutters were blown open as Armstrong mercilessly lashed him in a corner until the bell rang.

A heavy right landed on his ribs at the beginning of the sixth, and Sarron faced another surge. "Recovering somewhat," the *New York Times* reported, "Sarron jumped at Armstrong and traded willingly with him." Armstrong shot a left to the body and then launched an overhand right that crashed on the champion's jaw. Sarron "slumped to his knees and elbows," as if looking for a storm cellar under the ring, and was counted out.

Petey Sarron fought a total of one hundred and fifty-one times. He was stopped once. Armstrong called the signature shot that did it "the blackout."

The World Welterweight Title (May 31, 1938)

Armstrong's managers intended to take the three world championship belts in an orderly fashion, but Al Weill, manager of lightweight king Lou Ambers, asked for a rain check. Twelve pounds north, welterweight king Barney Ross wasn't about to give up a payday because of stormy weather. He accepted the challenge.

With a record of 72-3-3, Ross was an established master-boxer who, like Sarron, was never stopped. Born in New York City's Lower East Side, he stood second only to Benny Leonard among the celebrated Jewish champions who reigned from the 1910s through the 1930s and virtually disappeared after that. Barney Ross (nee Barnet David Rasofsky) was the last of the great ones.

As a welterweight, he had not been defeated since Jimmy McLarnin turned the trick back in 1934. Ross beat him before that bout and again after it. By the time he signed to face Armstrong, however, ennui had settled in because of the lack of challenges. He'd sneak tokes of a Chesterfield in the rubdown room and swig straight vodka at night after training. Not so this time. Ross's best fighting weight was one hundred and forty-two pounds, and that was precisely what the scale said at the weigh-in. It was also the contractual limit for the match.

Armstrong was having problems with the scale. Simply put, he was no welterweight. In a sport where participants ritualistically dried out, weighed in on the day of the fight, and then gorged at supper, Henry hurried to the scale with a belly full of water and beer, weighed in at only a hundred and thirty-three pounds, and made off for the nearest toilet.

The vast Jewish contingent in New York bet heavily on Ross, who entered the ring a seven-to-five favorite. The fistic fraternity was polled, and fifty of them favored Ross to outbox the smaller man. Thirty-six said he wouldn't.

Every radio in the Lower East Side was blaring when the great Jewish champion glided out of his corner at the opening bell. Working behind a jab and boxing at angles, Ross's eyes were wide open in the early rounds as he strained to measure the bobbing and weaving challenger. Armstrong's body attack was withering. He turned his fist around, crashed it into the champion's ribs, and mixed in left hooks and overhand rights. Ross's strategy was to step inside the eye of the storm—inside the looping shots, and shift Armstrong off balance. The strategy was masterfully executed, and Ross can be seen on film pivoting and turning Armstrong.

Unfortunately for Ross, two problems were becoming clear. First, he had assumed that his superior size would matter. It didn't. The second was a question of pace. Armstrong could keep a hellish pace indefinitely. Ross could not. By round seven, the featherweight champion was overpowering the welterweight champion. Ross was still throwing that right uppercut-left hook combination, but he was wavering like a weather vane in November.

It has become a convention among boxing historians to accede that the twenty-eight-year-old Ross got old in that bout, that he could no longer move as lively as he once did. That claim ignores what the film confirms: Armstrong's physical strength and pressure wore him out, just like it did Sarron. By the end of the tenth round, Ross was in big trouble.

Only his heart and Armstrong's sympathy allowed him to finish on his feet. Late in the fight, arguments abounded in both corners. Ross's chief second had the towel in hand and was ready to throw it in when Ross said, "—don't do it. I'm not quitting." The referee came over and Ross had to make a promise to alleviate the official's conscience. "Let me finish like a champion," he said, "and I promise I'll never fight again." In the other corner, Armstrong wanted to knock him out and be done with it. "I don't want to crucify him," he said. "I don't want to hurt him no more."

Armstrong would later claim that his seconds had gotten a signal to carry his opponent for the last four rounds, and that the two champions had a conversation during a clinch that went something like this:

Armstrong: "How you feel, Barney?"

Ross: "I'm dead."

Armstrong: "Jab and run, and I'll make it look good."

As the last bell ended the fight, Ross embraced his conqueror. "You're the greatest," he said. Close to it; Armstrong emerged from a battle against one of the finest boxers who ever lived with nothing more than a bruised knuckle.

The World Lightweight Title (August 17, 1938)

New York's Lou Ambers was as tough as old boots. Known as the "Herkimer Hurricane," he was a trainer's dream because the closest thing he had to a vice was going to the movies. Ambers was also a supremely skilled in-fighter whose pride still swelled his chest long after his retirement: "Oh Jesus," he would say. "I loved to fight."

A ringside view at the Ambers-Armstrong title fight in Madison Square Garden cost $16.50, same-day admission was $1.15, and soon eighteen thousand were fidgeting in the seats. A collision of two hurricanes was imminent. Would Armstrong surface with three simultaneous crowns? The odds said three-to-one that he would.

Al Jolson plunked down a grand that said Ambers wouldn't finish fifteen rounds. But Ambers was ready. "I'll cut up Henry Armstrong so badly," he predicted, "the referee will have to stop the fight." Reporters chewed on their pencils at this. "Don't worry about me," he snapped. "Wait until we've gone fifteen rounds and then ask Armstrong how he liked it."

The two champions were standing toe-to-toe and slugging it out for a full minute by round two as the crowd screamed and hats flew. Ambers clinched effectively inside and landed sneak shots, but it was Armstrong who caught him pulling back in the fifth with a long right. Ambers tumbled down. The referee counted to three when the bell rang, and his corner men rushed out to revive him. In the next round, Armstrong threw combinations that didn't end. Down went Ambers again.

He took an eight-count but nodded to his chief second, who by now had the spit bucket over his head.

Then Ambers found an answer: as Armstrong bent forward and barreled in, he stood his ground and shot uppercuts one after another. Armstrong hurled punches low, and the referee penalized him four rounds while Ambers knocked his mouthpiece out twice and severely split his lip. It was a war. In the fourteenth, Armstrong landed a right and Ambers reeled across the ring like a drunk chasing his hat, but he wouldn't go down again.

Armstrong said it was the "bloodiest fight I ever had in my life." The canvas, said Henry McLemore in press row, resembled a gigantic butcher's apron. "I'm not going to bleed no more," he promised the referee (who was close to stopping the fight), and then spat out his mouthpiece and got back to work. He ended up swallowing about a pint of his own blood along with the iodine and collodion used to congeal the cut in his mouth. Delirium set in sometime during round fifteen.

In Lou Amber's dressing room, McLemore suspected that the now ex-champion's screws were punched loose. Lou sat naked, covered with welts, his eye an egg, croaking the old favorite, "I Want a Girl Just Like the Girl That Married Dear Old Dad." Swaying to and fro, he was still ducking overhands that weren't coming anymore. "Whoop-a-doopy!" he said as McLemore made tracks for the other dressing room. Armstrong couldn't even remember the fifteenth round, much less the announcement of his great victory. His handlers would tell him later how they had to peel him off Ambers. A strange calm swept over him as he sat nursing a swollen left eye, five cuts over both eyes, and a mangled lip that would take fifteen stitches. Flashbulbs exploded in his face.

Hurricane Henry had reached his peak—the fistic equivalent of a category five. After storming three divisions and dethroning three champions in less than a year, the man was spent . . . but the boxing landscape would never be the same.

On 52nd Street the next morning, yellow cabs honk in traffic and clusters of pedestrians bustle to work outside Madison Square Garden. A gust carries a newspaper swirling through space and time until it lands at the feet of a gangly teenager in Central Park. The headline speaks to him. "TRIPLE CHAMPION!" it reads, and his eyes flash with ambition.

He finishes stretching and starts running down the winding bicycle path, against the wind.

HENRY ARMSTRONG'S SCORECARD

—25 points—
Quality of Opposition: 24.5

—15 points—
Ring Generalship: 14.5
Longevity: 14.6
Dominance: 15

—10 points—
Durability: 9.5
P/LO: 9.6
Intangibles: 9.5

Total *97.2*

*"Farewell to Sugar Ray" at Madison Square
Garden, 1965.* (Rogers Photo Archive)

The Second God of War

A *junk wagon pulled by a clopping nag lurches across 110th Street in New York City. Beside it walks a peddler whistling a Cab Calloway tune, his eyes jaundice yellow. In the distance, a gangly figure approaches out of Central Park. It is a young man about seventeen, boxing shadows in steady stride. He halts briefly and skips in place, shoulders hunched, chin down, and lets fly a shoe shine combination that ends with lightning left hooks. Spinning off the last of them, he runs on into Harlem, into the morning sun.*

In the afternoon, he heads over to Grupp's Gym on 116th Street. Old-time fighters loiter there, bound together by an uncommon past. "All they did was talk boxing," he would remember, "and all I did was listen." Harry Wills would teach him balance, Soldier Jones the difference a good jab can make. Among them is William Ward, who fought under a name dreaded in the 1920s—Kid Norfolk. Ward regales him with war stories about the blood-spattered men of a bygone era.

The phenomenon that was Sugar Ray Robinson began at the feet of masters and was forged from the inside out. The future was his.

Year One

He still had jumpy legs after his professional debut on the undercard of the Henry Armstrong-Fritzie Zivic title fight at Madison Square Garden. It was October 4, 1940. Showering quickly, he hurried upstairs from the dressing room to see his idol make the twentieth defense of the world welterweight title. What he saw he never forgot. Armstrong, the triple champion so many believed invincible, was bludgeoned, jabbed blind, and cracked with short shots until he had nothing left but courage. His conqueror was ruthless. "I pulled my trunks up and went to work on him," Zivic said. "I busted him up, cut him here and cut him there . . . when the eye was cut, I'd rub it with the laces to open it a little more."

In the cab ride home to Harlem, the young lightweight had vengeance on his mind. "Mom," he said. "I want to fight Zivic. I'll fix him for the way he beat Armstrong." His mother was having none of it—"Junior, I don't want you *ever* to fight Zivic."

Four days later, "Junior" was in Georgia to add a second-round technical knockout to his budding record, and after that he had matches in Philadelphia, Detroit, New Jersey, and Washington DC as often as three times a month. His opponents were unusually tough. His fifth was Norment Quarles, a one-time protégé of Jack Dempsey. Quarles had faced several champions in over a hundred professional bouts—yet couldn't finish half the eight scheduled rounds against this teenager. Robinson then headed back to the Garden to hand Oliver White his first stoppage loss in fifty fights.

In Philadelphia they say that even the winos know how to hook off a jab. Robinson was already good enough to flatten Philly fighters like they were grapes in a press. Jimmy Tygh, an aggressive lightweight who had not been stopped in sixty bouts was stopped twice, once cleanly and once after falling down five times. Mike Evans's career was in recovery when a left hook left him in a stupor in June 1941.

Robinson returned to Philadelphia only weeks later to risk his 20-0 record against a seasoned veteran with eighty fights, Sammy "The Clutch" Angott.

It should not have been so easy.

Robinson was expected to have trouble in close against a man with the fighting style of a squid, but he had answers. In the second round he sprang back and threw a looping right hand that parked on Angott's chin. Down went Angott. His eyelids were still fluttering when he got to his knees and then to his feet as the count reached nine. Robinson later claimed that the only reason Angott woke up was because his head was near the timekeeper's hammer as it pounded the count on the ring apron. Angott recovered enough to score left hooks to the body, but the long-range blasts were too much, and he lost a wide decision.

The victor, who had just turned twenty, was already being proclaimed as the best fighter in the world. And despite being the next logical challenger for Lew Jenkins' lightweight crown, it was Angott who got the title shot, and the title.

With an unconvincing crown atop his head, "The Clutch" whipped two top contenders and then got whipped himself for the second time against Robinson in a non-title bout. Angott tried him a third time a few years later and got whipped again.

By September 1941, the boxer the scribes were calling Ray "Sugar" Robinson faced undefeated U.S. sailor Marty Servo. Like Angott, Servo was the boss on the inside, but Robinson slid back and lit him up at range. To the delight of the Philadelphia crowd, Servo fought as if Robinson was an English king and he a cranky colonist. Unlike the Liberty Bell, Servo's head never cracked, but his revolution was thwarted.

On Halloween night, speed and talent glided into the ring at Madison Square Garden to confront Fritzie Zivic. The chance to avenge Henry Armstrong had, at last, arrived. Barney Nagler quipped that Robinson could box "as though he were playing the violin" but if Robinson had a violin, Zivic would have snatched it and broken it across his knees. "I'd give 'em the head, choke 'em, hit 'em in the balls . . . I used to bang 'em up pretty good," he said. "You're fighting, you're not playing the piano you know."

In the first round, Zivic scraped the inside of his gloves so hard against Robinson's face that Robinson thought the laces were steel wool. There was more to come. Zivic had a way of forcing his opponent to head butt himself: he'd loop his lead hand around the back of an opponent's neck in a clinch and jam his head on top of his own, then he'd looked to the referee with a phony plea in his eyes.

Robinson couldn't believe what was happening. At the end of the round, he flopped on the stool in his corner. Trainer George Gainford splashed him with a sponge and said, "Don't let him get close—keep him away with the jab." He did as he was told and won. Zivic was impressed: "Everything I done, he done better."

Not only did Robinson avenge his idol, he began to outshine him. Armstrong was fading while Robinson's learning curve became a straight line pointing to heaven. "Year One" saw twenty-six victories against a soon-to-be world lightweight champion, an undefeated future world welterweight champion, and a former world welterweight champion. Two of them were Hall of Famers in their prime. Robinson wasn't yet near his. He didn't have to be.

In December 1946, he would finally take his place on the welterweight throne. Jimmy Doyle would die at his hands six months later, and traumatized, Robinson would never again ignore his instincts or listen to anyone who disagreed with him. To insiders and former friends, he became a prima donna, out of reach and obsessed by self-interest. More than a few hated his guts though none could deny the greatness of a fighter whose record soared to a breathtaking 128-1-2 with eighty-four knockouts.

Sugar Ray Robinson is remembered for winning the world middleweight title five times, the first of which saw him destroy Jake LaMotta in an avant-garde performance; but those accomplishments aren't half the story. What prevented him from taking Joey Maxim's light heavyweight title on a scorching summer day in 1952 was nothing human. With an insurmountable lead on the scorecards after thirteen rounds, he collapsed with heat stroke.

"God wanted me to lose!" a delirious Robinson said in the dressing room at Yankee Stadium. "God beat me!"

The truth wasn't far off.

Had circumstances—boxing politics and the weather, been different, might he have been the first and only fighter in history to take the lightweight, welterweight, middleweight, and light heavyweight thrones? The answer forces a startling realization: despite all his accolades, the man born Walker Smith Jr. is even greater than we know.

Year Twenty-Five

"Whom Fortune wishes to destroy," Publilius Syrus wrote, "she first makes mad." At forty-four years old, Sugar Ray was preparing for his two-hundredth professional bout. It was 1965. "I am telling you I am going to win the title again," he insisted. He planned to do it the old-fashioned way, though fourth-rated Joey Archer would prove to be a slippery stepping stone.

The books had Robinson a two-to-one underdog in what was going to be his fourteenth fight that year. Nat Fleischer watched him lose four times since May and said what is always said at the end of a boxer's professional life: "His legs are gone." But they still looked good, and he still had that aura of beautiful danger as he ascended into the ring, conked and svelte like the days of old.

Robinson knew better. Aging ex-champions always know—even when they lie to themselves or go mad with delusions. Grandeur seems to dangle over their graying heads like a star on a string, but they can't jump anymore to reach it, and their gloves, like arthritic hands, can no longer hold it. It all slips away until the earth-bound god-in-denial is publically humiliated.

As the bell tolled the end of ten one-sided rounds in Pittsburgh's Civic Arena, a battered Robinson embraced Archer. Archer escorted him to his corner, and the old fighter stood facing it with his head bowed. And then something happened. Fans at ringside who had been hollering "Joey! Don't hit him!" over the last few rounds began standing up and drifting over to Sugar Ray's corner. First a few and then dozens gathered beneath him, applauding with reverence. Robinson's eyes met theirs, and the ovation washed over him. His defeat was being sanctified.

Fickle Fortune had changed her mind. This fighter would not be condemned to humiliation, not now, not ever.

The next afternoon he was stretched across a bed at the Carlton House Hotel, his aching head propped up on a pillow. Did the expression on his face indicate contentment or resignation? Perhaps it was both. No man had ever stopped him, but the time had come to stop himself. With reporters scribbling on notepads, he quietly concluded his career.

The director of boxing at Madison Square Garden called him a few weeks later. "Ray," he said, "it just doesn't seem right that a man of your stature should be allowed to retire so quietly . . . we'd like to throw a farewell party for you that will pay you the tribute you deserve." It was dubbed "Farewell to Sugar Ray" and scheduled just before the main event on December 10.

"He's the greatest fighter there ever was, and for me that's saying something," Muhammad Ali said that night. "When I was a little kid, I'd watch Sugar Ray Robinson on the TV, and when I started fightin' I copied his moves . . . and I still do. When I go into the ring now, he's on my mind."

The crowd was on its feet as he made his way down the aisle. They were still cheering when he climbed into the same ring where he began his career a quarter century before, where he avenged an idol and became a greater one.

Four former middleweight kings were announced and stood in the corners surrounding their common opponent. Among them were Carmen Basilio, Gene Fullmer, Carl "Bobo" Olson, and Randy Turpin who flew in all the way from England. Barbara Long of the *Village Voice* mused that they "could have rushed him and got him good," and "tough old Carmen looked like he was entertaining the thought." They closed in on him slowly, warily, and lifted him up. Sugar Ray's smile reflected the lights, and he extended his open hands not unlike a messiah.

At the end, he stood alone in a spotlight, his terrycloth robe dazzling white. All were moved. The African Americans scattered throughout the crowd were more than moved. For them it was a spiritual experience. The man had his faults, to be sure, but the image of this champion was a reflection of something larger than himself—the strength and passion and brilliance of his people. It still is.

With tears streaming down his face, he began to speak, and then faltered. A young man in the crowd was heard to whisper, "Talk to me, daddy." An elderly man said, "Let us hear you son," and wept openly. The boxer's voice trembled as he spoke into the microphone: "I'll miss the applause that makes a guy get up off that stool one more time."

Ducking his head, Sugar Ray Robinson slipped through maroon ropes that served as boundaries for his kingdom. He stood on the apron staring at the top rope for a moment, then kissed it and descended from the ring.

The gods themselves throw incense.

SUGAR RAY ROBINSON'S SCORECARD

—25 points—
Quality of Opposition: 24.6

—15 points—
Ring Generalship: 15
Longevity: 14.9
Dominance: 14.8

—10 points—
Durability: 9.7
P/LO: 9.2
Intangibles: 9.6

Total *97.8*

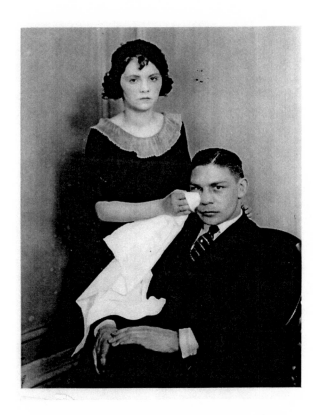

The Pittsburgh Windmill with wife Mildred after
defeating Tommy Gibbons at Madison Square Garden.
(March, 15, 1922)

The God of War

Next him . . . [a] scepter'd king,
Stood up, the strongest and the fiercest spirit
. . . now fiercer by despair.
—*Paradise Lost*, bk II, 1.44

April 29, 1924, Boston. *Trolleys spark and screech as they rumble
down the split on Huntington Avenue. Fedoras bob past the Boston-
Albany Railroad yard and darkened storefronts, emerge from Model Ts,
and hurry across the street after dinner at Sunning Restaurant. Everyone
seems to converge at the main entrance of the Mechanics Building where
they funnel in like sand through an hourglass. Inside the sprawling Victorian façade is a great hall. There, beneath the balconies and sloping
orchestra sections, a boxing ring looms in the light. The buzzing crowd
glances downward as they squeeze between rows.*

Tension is building around the empty ring.

Three preliminary bouts opened the program that cool spring
evening. Local boys duked it out until bragging rights belonged to
Somerville, East Boston, and South Boston. Chances are excellent
that all six of them were white. William Ward wasn't. He was as
black as Newgate's knocker, and about as ominous as the old English
prison behind it. At the age that others were building forts in the
woods or playing stick ball in the street, he was blindfolded, fighting
and bleeding against a dozen other black boys in battles royal. As an
adult, he lived to knock heads—black, white and every hue in the
middle in undocumented contests before punching his way through

167

the professional ranks.

He was dangerous, this man who fought under the name "Kid Norfolk." He trained at Grupp's Gym on 116th Street in New York and was a superior counterpuncher with a piston jab. His back was a wall, his legs stout, and he understood leverage as well as any future juggernaut. Despite blasting his way up to the third rung of the light heavyweight ladder, insiders already knew that Gene Tunney wasn't going near him. Hall of Famers Billy Miske and Tiger Flowers took a risk and were defeated. Former white hopes Arthur Pelkey and Gunboat Smith joined them.

Standing only five feet nine, he was strong enough to whip Big Bill Tate three times, and Tate was over six feet six and two hundred thirty-five pounds. Only five months earlier, Kid Norfolk manhandled the world-famous Battling Siki before a crowd of twelve thousand at Madison Square Garden. By fight's end Siki was choking on his own blood.

Every eye in the house is on him as he emerges into view and walks down the aisle, deadly serious. He is aware of the crowd's thoughts, their prejudices, but after putting his life on the line ninety-six times in similar venues, he has learned to disconnect fear. Kid Norfolk stands in the middle of the ring bowing low to the crowd . . . then waits.

Two nights before, Norfolk stepped off the train at South Station where a large contingent of African Americans from the South End waited for him. The middleweight champion of the world was on the same train. His name was Harry Greb. He probably saw the cheering crowd as he walked by unnoticed, carrying his own bags. Like Norfolk, he was unconcerned about crowds or weight divisions and found it amusing to attack someone he stood eyes-to-chest with. Greb had thrashed about fourteen heavyweights already. Within two months he too would face a fighter who stood six feet six, and win every round.

These two giant-killers had already crossed paths three years earlier in what one local paper called "one of the fastest and most grueling" battles Pittsburgh ever saw. Norfolk outweighed Greb by seventeen pounds and landed shots with such force that the iron-jawed champion was spinning on Queer Street in the opening minutes. A manager of a preliminary boxer who had come upstairs for the main event was astonished: "Never before have I seen two first-rate boxers rip and tear as they did," he recounted to reporters. "How Greb ever survived that first round is beyond me." Norfolk dropped Greb in the third "like a sack of oats," and both men were cut and bleeding as they came out for the last round. But that was the least of it. The victory may have cost Greb an eye.

In those days, boxing gloves resembled leather mittens. They weighed about five ounces and had movable thumbs. Biographer Bill Paxton identified Greb-Norfolk I as the fight where the Pittsburgh native first suffered an injury to his retina. Medical science hadn't advanced enough to prevent eventual blindness, so Greb kept it a secret and fought on, ruthlessly, to offset his handicap. He had forty bouts afterward and defeated three of the greatest light heavyweights who ever lived, ruining the virgin records of Tommy Gibbons (39-0-1) and Gene Tunney (41-0-1), and defeating the great "Phantom of Philly," Tommy Loughran. The right field of his vision was swimming when he did. By the time he arrived in Boston for the rematch against Kid Norfolk, he was completely blind in his right eye.

No one else knew what Norfolk had done. But Greb did.

The middleweight champion walks toward the ring, steps up the stairs, and slips through the ropes. A corner man stands behind him and takes his robe as the fighter scuffs the soles of his shoes in the resin box. Greb is wearing green trunks, his hair in well-oiled retreat from the mug below.

Had he stayed employed at Westinghouse and become an electrician, Greb may have been passable as a Rudolph Valentino stand-in. As it was, old scar tissue swelled his eyebrows, his nose had more dents than a backyard jalopy, and the rare times that he smiled for a photograph he looked like he was about to eat your liver with fava beans. Valentino may have had the "look-at-me" physique of a movie star, but the cabled muscles up and down Greb's arms made it clear what he was—a fighter not a lover.

He was also a widower. The night he faced Norfolk for the second time marked thirteen months and one day since his wife Mildred died at home in Pittsburgh. He stood at her bedside, watching her go.

Referee Jack Sheehan stands between both fighters and eyes them nervously. Both Greb and Norfolk look right through Sheehan, one glaring at the other, and the other glaring back. They know who the threat is in this ring, and the bespectacled guy in the middle, in the way, ain't it.

What follows is less a boxing contest than a pier-six brawl. The most feared light heavyweight in the world rushes out of his corner and forces Greb into the ropes. Greb clips him with a short hook to the chin. They clinch. Norfolk's strategy becomes clear early: he's shooting to the body to slow Greb's demon speed. Two go south of the beltline. Regis Welsh of the Pittsburgh Post *is ringside watching Greb retaliate "by clubbing and mauling [Norfolk] about." In the second round Greb is swarming all over his man from every angle and turns Norfolk around with lefts and rights to the body. Suddenly, Norfolk puts his head down and charges, ramming Greb headlong through the ropes and out of the ring. He lands sideways in the press section.*

The crowd is beside itself as Greb climbs back into the ring and tears into Norfolk. In the third, Greb realizes that Norfolk is too strong and tries boxing at range, jabbing hard and landing the better shots, though he is still being forced backward. Things get bad in the fourth round. State boxing officials in attendance don't know what to do—both men are "wrestling, clubbing, charging, and butting" and the referee is losing control.

The African American's mouth is running red as the fifth begins, and the crowd is standing on chairs yelling, "Let 'em fight the way they want!" Norfolk bangs the left side of Greb's ribs while Greb attacks at full speed.

Welsh watches Norfolk hook three shots to Greb's groin, though Greb carries on as if waiting for a chance to get even. Norfolk is now holding and hitting as Greb tries to wrest free and attack from the outside. Soon Greb is doing it too, grabbing Norfolk by the neck and punching the daylights out of him with his free hand.

The bell—which Welsh notes might have been salvaged from some old church belfry, clangs, and Norfolk throws a left hook anyway. Greb responds in kind before walking back to his corner, looking menacingly over his shoulder.

The old church bell clangs again. Norfolk drives the smaller man to the ropes, and Greb spins off and lands a combination. Norfolk again tries to physically prevent him from getting outside, holding and whacking away while Greb mauls and maneuvers. The referee is impotent. After the sixth round ends, Norfolk half-turns toward his corner and unleashes a right hand. It's a flagrant foul and the third such offense. Greb has had enough. Enraged, he whirls in with punches flying while Norfolk gets down low and rips shots to the body. A pop bottle flies in from a balcony and shatters at their feet as state officials and policemen jump into the ring to break the fighters up and escort them to their corners.

The great hall shakes as thousands of feet stamp, and the largest indoor crowd in Boston to date howls to the rafters. Greb is content. He knows he won at least four of the first six rounds. The referee seems to climb out from under the ring and hastily announces Norfolk as the winner "due to a foul by Greb"—then flees the scene. A wave of humanity surges forward demanding to know what happened. The boxing commissioner stands up to calm the crowd. He announces that it was Norfolk, not Greb who was "the real offender" and plans to override the verdict.

Meanwhile, Norfolk takes his gloves off and moves toward Greb, who is still seated on his stool.

Greb gets up to meet him . . .

Greb got up to meet him. As rough as he was on anyone who got into the ring with him, Greb's willingness to fight African-Americans on equal terms was remarkable. Tommy Loughran and Gene Tunney were not so willing; both consistently upheld the so-called color line in vogue at the time. Jack Dempsey declined to risk the heavyweight title against a black man, despite his posturing about fighting Harry Wills. Jack Johnson himself ducked contenders who shared his complexion when he was champion. Greb was a glaring exception. The middleweight king was not only half-blind; he was colorblind. "All men," he may have quipped, "bleed equal."

The next morning's dailies declared his clash with Kid Norfolk to be "one of the toughest, roughest, and ugliest battles ever staged here or elsewhere." A breathless Regis Welsh called it the "grandest, roughest, go-as-you-please milling anyone has ever seen anywhere."

For Greb, it was nothing new. He turned professional in 1913, when boxing only wished it could crawl up from the sewer into the red-light district. Hell-raisers like Battling Nelson and Ad Wolgast fought that year, after going forty rounds in perhaps the most vicious brawl of the twentieth century. Leather mittens, no groin protectors, no mouth guards, twenty rounds—there were few cuties in the sport.

Greb came out of that era enduring hardships that would dissuade many boxers today from leaving the dressing room.

Early in his career he was kneed in the genitals during a bout and had to be carried from the ring. He was once assaulted by a corner man, and bitten on the glove by a frustrated opponent who plum ran out of ways to cope with his windmill attack. Another opponent's teeth missed his glove and clamped on his arm. A headcase entered the ring with a live boa constrictor draped around his neck and then proceeded to aim for his eyes with both thumbs.

Greb would fight despite injuries that included broken hands and broken arms. He was once punched low so hard that he vomited over the side of the ring; he passed out, woke up and refused to claim victory on a foul, finished the fight, and won all ten rounds. He fought a heavyweight while sporting a black eye and two boils from a fight two days earlier, and won nine of the ten rounds. In 1916, he fought the second round against Kid Graves after the radius in his left arm had been broken in half. "His arm was so bent, his left jab was really a left hook," a handler recalled. He was winning the round when his corner begged the referee to stop the ghastly spectacle.

The year after he faced Kid Norfolk in Boston, he fought not only his opponent but the referee as well. The referee was Marvin Hart, former world heavyweight champion. Greb was arrested and fined $100.

Trolling three divisions looking for fights over a thirteen-year career, he got them—three hundred of them. That's two thousand, five hundred ninety professional rounds—three times as many as Roberto Duran and more than Julio Cesar Chavez, Oscar De La Hoya, Pernell Whitaker, Ray Leonard, Larry Holmes, and Lennox Lewis combined. The heads that sat on his mantle included twelve world champions, nineteen title-holders, and fifteen inductees of the International Boxing Hall of Fame.

He was a formless fighter of the nightmarish strain. In his prime, opponents found themselves beset on all sides by what seemed to be three attackers at once. When punched at, he seemed to be nowhere, but when punching, he seemed to be everywhere.

No film of Greb in action has been found to date, but there is the testimony of witnesses. John Van Swearingen, who died in 1983, worked as a second in Greb's corner in the early 1920s. He never forgot the spectacle of Greb's shots coming in so ferociously and "with such accelerated velocity that you could not see the punches being thrown." All that anyone in the audience could see "was the head of the opponent ratcheting backwards from three to five times incrementally." Swearingen tells posterity that Greb was "absolutely the most lightning fast man with his fists that I, or anyone else I've ever talked with, has ever seen."

Forty minutes after the second war between Greb and Norfolk, the great hall of Boston's Mechanics Building is quiet. A janitor pushes a broom before crumpled programs, whistling "Tin Roof Blues." Two officials stand murmuring at ringside, one of them running his fingers up under his hat. He shakes his head in disbelief at the night's carnage and the other sniffs a response, his shoe grinding the end of a cigarette into the floor. They bid each other goodnight and depart.

An invisible hand switches off the lights. A full moon peers through arched windows cutting the darkness and illuminating dust. Footsteps fade and then a door clangs shut, echoing off elegant walls.

The boxing ring looms in the stillness, a pagan shrine splashed with blood.

HARRY GREB'S SCORECARD
—25 points—
Quality of Opposition: 25

—15 points—
Ring Generalship: 15
Longevity: 15
Dominance: 14.9

—10 points—
Durability: 10
P/LO: 10
Intangibles: 10

Total *99.9*

OUT OF THE PAST

Out of the Past

The Italianate courtyard of the Boston Public Library is a secret place for scholars and students. Marble arches and stone corridors form a square reminiscent of Rome's Palazzo della Cancelleria. There's a vision rising out of the fountain in the center, a nude sculpture called *Bacchante and Infant Faun*. Condemned during the Victorian era, it depicts wanton revelry in honor of the god of wine.

On Thursday, I sat on one of the ornate chairs before an ornate table and gazed upon another vision, this one fully clothed and at study. Torrents of ash blonde hair kept spilling forward over her open book. She'd throw it over a shoulder. It fell again. She tucked it behind an ear. It untucked and launched itself back onto the page. The fifth time she threw it back, she bristled. I was tickled. When she packed her things and rose out of her chair like a bacchante in a blue dress, she glanced my way. There were about six steps between us, which meant that I had about six seconds to find words that struck the right balance between confident and cute. As it happened, nothing happened. I choked, she breezed by, and all I got was a sideways look; *il maloccio*.

Boston has secret places only the locals know. You won't find them in a car. You'd be better off on a horse. This city wasn't planned on a grid like New York or Washington; it wasn't planned at all.

Ralph Waldo Emerson said that cows did the urban planning, and he wasn't wrong enough. "In Boston town of old renown," an old postcard reads, "the gentle cows the pathways made, which grew to streets that keep strangers quite dismayed." It is best explored on foot.

After a few minutes repairing chipped pride, I left the Palazzo and walked through the ritzy Back Bay.

The Mechanics Building stood around the corner on Huntington Avenue and hosted hundreds of boxing matches. One of them involved Harry Greb and Kid Norfolk in 1924. It ended after the referee disqualified the wrong guy, at least according to the crowd that almost tore the place apart. The match was trumpeted by the dailies as "the fastest and most curious contest ever in a Boston ring." In 1959, the building was razed to make way for the Prudential Plaza—to make way for flaccid modernity. The site of Greb and Norfolk's pier-six brawl is now a *reflecting pool*.

I walked down Boylston Street toward what was once the Combat Zone, past the site of the Gilded Cage, a gaudy strip club managed in the 1940s by a former champion from the 1920s named Johnny Wilson.

Born Giovanni Panica, Wilson was a Sicilian-American out of Charlestown and never out of connections. With friends like mob bosses Al Capone and Frank Costello, why should he be? For three years he ducked Greb to stay connected to his crown. When Greb finally cornered him, he hammered Wilson's overhanging nose for fifteen rounds and took that crown.

Another middleweight named Jock Malone was confident that he could do to Wilson what Greb did—so confident, in fact, that he promised the press that he would jump into Boston Harbor if he lost. Wilson knocked him out. The next day, a crowd of thousands gathered at the Charlestown Bridge to see if he'd keep his word. Malone arrived on time. He climbed over the railing and posed for a moment, fully dressed and wearing a straw hat. "I owe Wilson a splash!" he called out before plunging fifty feet into the brine. Boston cheered as he swam ashore and hopped into a waiting car.

Wilson lost five of his next seven and hung up the gloves. During the tail end of Prohibition, he ran a speakeasy in New York and acquired a taste for cigars and sleeping until noon. Later, he returned to Boston and managed a marathon dance in Somerville, the Swanee Grille in Roxbury, a bookstore on the corner of Massachusetts Avenue and Gainsborough Street, and assorted nightclubs around the city. He managed a burlesque sensation and booked her at the Gilded Cage: Sally Keith was known as the "Queen of the Tassel Tossers" for her uncanny ability to swing tassels dangling from her bosoms in opposite directions.

By the time I was born, Wilson was pushing eighty and still had black hair parted down the middle and slicked back, Roaring Twenties style. In the evening he'd have a glass of burgundy, light up a cigar, and walk these same crooked streets for hours on end, reminiscing.

I went left at Boylston Square, maneuvering my way through artsy types and Emerson College students in flip-flops. The Paramount Theatre approached out of the past.

When it was built during the Hoover administration, the Paramount was a movie house, one of the first of its kind, all class. By the time Nixon got in, it was a dilapidated creep joint, all crass. The only white guys at this end of Washington Street wore raincoats, and the rest didn't even pretend to be part of civil society. Sharp ones with sharp eyes scanned for easy marks. The broken ones lay down in dark corners. By the 1980s they were lying around on the sidewalks too, and young hoodlums like me couldn't even maintain a respectable swagger without stepping over them.

The Paramount reopened last year, all class once again. A seven thousand-bulb marquee lights up Washington Street every night like a dream. Like a great comeback.

As the evening sky turned orange and then dimmed, I was in the North End, the old Italian enclave just a stone's throw from Faneuil Hall. The Fisherman's Feast, a tradition brought from Sicily to these shores a hundred years ago, was underway. A crowd was carrying a statue of the Madonna down to Christopher Columbus Park to bless the waters. Heralded by a marching band, the procession winded its way back to a chapel where the statue rested. Green, white, and red confetti littered streets that were lined with carts hawking salsicce, arancini, pizza, and, best of all, cannoli from Mike's Pastry. A gypsy offered handwriting analysis. A master of ceremonies sat in a booth and heckled the yuppies who didn't buy raffle tickets. "You wit tha green shirt!" I heard him say to one of them. "Buy a raffle ticket! Where you goin'? *Where you goin'?*"

Local boxing legend Tony DeMarco was there. It was his night.

Unlike fellow Siciliano Johnny Wilson, DeMarco was born in Boston. He never left the North End. Way back in 1955, he became the shortest welterweight champion with the longest nickname: "Short, Dark, and Harmful." He lost the title to a fiercer Italian in Carmen Basilio, though he never lost his friends. They all came out this evening to see him honored by the Madonna del Soccorso di Sciacca Society as the "Italian-American of the Year."

Carrying a water bottle in his hand, he climbed the stairs onto a makeshift stage as if it was a ring. He's pushing eighty now. Despite the busted beak and heavy scarring around the brows, I saw no signs of impairment, no sobering reminders of those twenty-four rounds with Basilio that would have killed lesser men.

When he took the microphone, he offered no war stories. He spoke instead of love and friendship. His father was from the fisherman's town of Sciacca in Sicily, his mother was too—"God bless her soul"—so this feast is close to his heart. "I know they see me now," he said, his voice breaking. "I am as proud to receive this award as I was when I became welterweight champion of the world." His arms spread wide as if to embrace the cheering crowd. Camera phones clicked where once flashbulbs fired.

It was getting late when I sat on an ornate chair before an ornate table in front of Caffè Vittoria. Hanover Street still bustled with tourists looking for secret places and a hint of the North End's sto-ried past. I sipped espresso.

Boston is a sentimental city. It's a city that holds onto yesterday so tightly that even its new glories are often old glories restored, if only for a night.

I walked back toward Boylston Square . . . and wished I had a cigar.

August 22, 2011

APPENDIX

The Thirty Greatest Fighters of the Modern Era

THE GREATEST FIGHTERS OF THE MODERN ERA: 1st - 10th

Rank	Boxer	Quality of Opposition (25)	Ring Generalship (15)	Longevity (15)	Dominance (15)	Durability (10)	P/Larger Opponents (10)	Intangibles (10)	Total
1st	Harry Greb	25	15	15	14.9	10	10	10	99.9
2nd	Sugar Ray Robinson	24.6	15	14.9	14.8	9.7	9.2	9.6	97.8
3rd	Henry Armstrong	24.5	14.5	14.6	15	9.5	9.6	9.5	97.2
4th	Ezzard Charles	24.6	15	14.5	14.9	8	10	9.8	96.8
5th	Roberto Duran	24.1	14.7	14.8	14.9	9.8	9.7	8.5	96.5
6th	Archie Moore	24.7	14.6	15	14.8	8	9.6	9.7	96.4
7th	Mickey Walker	24.4	14.4	14.6	14.5	8.6	10	9.7	96.2
8th	Benny Leonard	24.3	15	14.7	15	8.7	8.2	9.6	95.5
9th	Willie Pep	24	15	14.8	14.9	8.2	7.5	9.4	93.8
10th	Charley Burley	24.3	14.5	13.2	12.5	10	9.4	9.7	93.6

184

THE GREATEST FIGHTERS OF THE MODERN ERA: 11th - 20th

Rank	Boxer	Quality of Opposition (25)	Ring Generalship (15)	Longevity (15)	Dominance (15)	Durability (10)	P/Larger Opponents (10)	Intangibles (10)	Total
11th	Barney Ross	24.2	14.7	12.7	14.7	9.3	8.4	9.5	93.5
12th	Muhammad Ali	23.5	14.3	13.3	14.9	8.9	8.9	9.5	93.3
13th	Joe Louis	23.8	14.1	13.4	15	8.4	9.4	9.1	93.2
14th	Tony Canzoneri	24.6	14.2	14.4	14.5	9.8	5.8	9.8	93.1
15th	Ike Williams	24.1	14.1	14.2	13.9	8.3	9.0	9.3	92.9
16th	Billy Conn	24	14.4	12.4	14	8.8	9.8	9.4	92.8
17th	Julio Cesar Chavez	23.2	14.1	14.2	14.9	9.3	8.3	8.7	92.7
18th	Kid Gavilan	24	14.1	13.9	13.6	9.8	8.2	9	92.6
19th	Holman Williams	23.8	14.8	14.4	12.1	9.2	8.8	9	92.5
20th	Sandy Saddler	23.7	14.4	14.3	13.9	9.6	7.2	9.1	92.2

THE GREATEST FIGHTERS OF THE MODERN ERA: 21ˢᵗ -30ᵗʰ

Rank	Boxer	Quality of Opposition (25)	Ring Generalship (15)	Longevity (15)	Dominance (15)	Durability (10)	P/Larger Opponents (10)	Intangibles (10)	Total
21ˢᵗ	Emile Griffith	23.3	14.1	14.2	13.9	8.6	8.6	9.4	92.1
22ⁿᵈ	Jose Napoles	22.4	14.8	12.9	14.7	9.4	8.5	9.3	92
23ʳᵈ	Kid Chocolate	24	14.7	14	14.7	9	6	9.4	91.8
24ᵗʰ	Pernell Whitaker	22.9	15	11.9	14.8	8.3	9.4	9.2	91.5
25ᵗʰ	Jimmy Bivins	24.5	14	13.3	12.4	8.7	9.5	9	91.4
26ᵗʰ	Tiger Flowers	24.3	14.4	14.3	12.5	7.2	9.4	9.2	91.3
27ᵗʰ	Eder Jofre	22	14.5	13.5	14.4	9.5	8	9.3	91.2
28ᵗʰ	Thomas Hearns	23.8	14.2	13.3	13.9	7.7	9.2	9	91.1
29ᵗʰ	Billy Graham	23.7	14.4	13.9	11.4	9.8	7.9	9.4	90.5
30ᵗʰ	Jake LaMotta	24.1	13.9	13.2	12.5	9.9	8	8.8	90.4

186

Sources and Acknowledgments

Earlier versions of most of the essays in this book appeared in TheSweet-Science.com.

"The Immortals: Jewish Fighters Ancient and Modern": Josephus's *The Jewish Wars*, and Martin Hengel's *The Zealots: Investigations into the Jewish Freedom Movement in the Period From Herod I until 70 A.D.* (Copyright © 1989 T&T Clark Ltd.) were useful as resources. James P. Dawson's account of the Palestine Fund Show in Madison Square Garden appeared in the *New York Times*. Douglas Century's commendable *Barney Ross* (Copyright © 2006 by Douglas Century) was also useful. Charley Phil Rosenberg's story in Peter Heller's *In This Corner: 42 World Champions Tell Their Stories*. Copyright © 1973 by Peter Heller. Ray Arcel's comments in Ronald K. Fried's *Corner Men: Great Boxing Trainers*. Copyright © 1991 by Ronald K. Fried. The "song" is excerpted from Psalm 56.

"Fireworks and Falling Giants": Citations referring to the American Revolution in Benson Bobrick's *Angel in the Whirlwind: The Triumph of the American Revolution*. Copyright © 1997 by Benson Bobrick. Gunboat Smith's recollections in Heller's *In This Corner*.

"Kid Chocolate²": Details regarding Kid Chocolate and his fights derived from Wilbur Wood's interview with manager Pincho Gutierrez in the *New York Sun*; *Milwaukee Journal*, 4 January 1929;

"Ez Story: Clothes Make the Man," *New York Times* (15 June 1954); "Tony Takes KO Over Chocolate" 25 November 1933 by Herbert W. Barker (AP) and "Canzoneri Stops Chocolate in Second Round K.O" 25 November 1933 by Edward J. Neil (AP). Henry Armstrong's comment recorded in Peter Heller's *In This Corner* (Copyright © 1994 by Peter Heller). Special thanks to Peter "Kid Chocolate" Quillin for granting an interview for this essay.

"Alexis Arguello": Special thanks to Ray Mancini.

"Force of Will": Background information about Joe Frazier in Jack Griffin's "Frazier Still Dreaming as Ali Started His Climb," *Pittsburgh Press* (3 March 1971), and "Catching Up With Smokin Joe Frazier," by Sabina Clark in *Irish Edition* (12 June 2009). Descriptions of Frazier's "joy" in battle found in *New York Times* (20 July 1967 and 26 June 1969). Eddie Futch's recollections found in Ronald K. Fried's *Corner Men* (pp. 312-313) and Dave Anderson's *In The Corner* (pp. 246-247).

"The Liston Chronicles": A few of the Liston war stories found in Nick Tosches' *The Devil and Sonny Liston*. Copyright © 2000 by Nick Tosches. Information regarding Malcolm X and Elijah Muhammad derived from *The Autobiography of Malcolm X* (Copyright © 1965 by Malcolm X and Alex Haley) and "New Muslims," a publication by the Islamic Educational, Scientific, and Cultural Organization (ISESCO). Floyd Patterson's statements in an HBO Sports Special called "Sonny Liston: The Mysterious Life and Death of a Champion." "Liston was the Devil" was found in Tosches work. Contemporary articles from *New York Times* and *Boston Globe* were also used for this series. Special thanks to Nick Gamble for his assistance with THE RING ratings.

"A Birthday for Sonny Liston": "Should Patterson Give Title Shot to Liston: Sonny's 'Rebirth' to Help," Larry Still (*Jet*, 10 October 1961); Jack McKinney's "He's Mad and Getting Madder" (*Sports*

Illustrated, 24 September 1962), Jack Olsen's "What's Become of the Big Bear?" (*SI*, 13 May 1968) and William Nack's "O Unlucky Man" (*SI*, 4 February 1991), Evans Kirkby's article in the *Milwaukee Journal* (24 May 1965), A.S. Young's *Sonny Liston: The Champ Nobody Wanted* (Copyright © 1963 by A.S. Young), THE RING, September 1967, Nick Tosches' *The Devil and Sonny Liston*, UPI-AP "Sought Floyd Rematch" (6 January 1971), Rob Sneed's *Sonny Liston: His Life, Strife, and the Phantom Punch* (Copyright © 2008 by Rob Sneed), and U.S. Census reports (1860, 1870, 1930, 1940) were resources for this essay.

The Gods of War series has fingerprints on it that deserve to be acknowledged. These include, but are not limited to, boxing historians Danny Trihas, Matt McGrain, and Dan Workman. BoxRec.com was an excellent resource.

"The Tenth God of War": Sparring match with Elmer Ray as recalled by Howard Branson in Allen S. Rosenfeld's *Charley Burley: The Life and Hard Times of an Uncrowned Champion*, pp. 492-493. Copyright © 2000, 2002, 2003 by Allen S. Rosenfeld. The JD Turner bout recounted in Harry Otty's *Charley Burley and the Black Murderers' Row*, pp. 152-153. Copyright © 1995-2006 by Harry Otty. Armstrong's avoidance of Burley found on p. 84. Zivic's buying his contract found on p. 121. Archie Moore's statements found in *Any Boy Can: The Archie Moore Story* (Copyright © 1971 Archie Lee Moore and Leonard B. Pearl) and Marilyn G. Douroux's *Archie Moore: The Ole Mongoose: The Authorized Biography of the Undefeated Light Heavyweight Champion of the World*. Copyright © 1991 by Marilyn G. Douroux.

"The Ninth God of War": Memories of Stillman's Gym found in Ronald K. Fried's essay "Stillman's Gym" in *Corner Men. Friday's Heroes*, by Willie Pep and Robert Sacchi (Copyright © 2008 Robert Sacchi), was also used as a resource. Lou Stillman's quotes found in his obituary in *New York Times* (20 August 1969). See also James B. Dawson's coverage of the Wright and Saddler II fights for *New York Times*. Pep's injuries after the plane crash recorded in *Harford Courant* (16 January 1947).

"The Eighth God of War": The author is indebted to the National Museum of American Jewish History's "Sting Like a Maccabee: The Golden Age of the American Jewish Boxer" exhibition, as well as Allen Bodner's *When Boxing was a Jewish Sport* (Copyright © 1997 by Allen Brodner), and Douglas Century's *Barney Ross*. Ray Arcel's memories are recorded in Ronald K. Fried's *Corner Men*.

"The Seventh God of War": *Mickey Walker: The Toy Bulldog and His Times* by Mickey Walker with Joe Reichler (Copyright © 1961 by Joe Reichler and Edward P. Walker) and Peter Heller's interview of Walker in *In This Corner* were useful for this essay. "Forgotten Hollywood: Ace Hudkins . . . boxer, stuntman, Batman, and Trigger" by E.J. Fleming; Westbrook Pegler's column in *Chicago Daily Tribune*, Eddie Muller's column in *San Francisco Examiner*, Joe William's column in *Pittsburgh Press,* Furman Bisher's column in *Atlanta Journal,* and Paul Lowry and Frank Roche's columns in *Los Angeles Times*. Doc Kearns recollection of the Swiderski melee found in an interview by Prescott Sullivan (*San Francisco Examiner*, 12 February 1948).

"The Sixth God of War": Information not otherwise acknowledged in this article was derived from Archie Moore's obituary in *New York Times*, his autobiography with Leonard B. Pearl *Any Boy Can: The Archie Moore Story*, Marilyn G. Douroux's *Archie Moore: The Ole Mongoose*, Mike Fitzgerald's *The Ageless Warrior: The Life of Boxing Legend Archie Moore* (Copyright © 2004 by Mike Fitzgerald), THE RING's interview with Jimmy Bivins (June 1996), *New York Times* (28 December 1952), and Frank Deford's "Ageless Warrior" in *Sports Illustrated* (8 May 1989).

"The Fifth God of War": The author is indebted to Pete Hamill, Michael Katz, and Dave Anderson for their coverage of the Duran-Leonard bout in June 1980. Ronald K. Fried's *Corner Men*, Anderson's *In the Corner: Great Boxing Trainers Talk About Their Art* (Copyright © 1991 by Dave Anderson) and George Kimball's *Four Kings: Leonard, Hagler, Hearns, Duran and the Last Great Era of Boxing* (Copyright © 2008 by George Kimball) were valuable resources.

"The Fourth God of War": Dave Anderson's *In the Corner* and his collaboration with Sugar Ray Robinson on *Sugar Ray: The Sugar Ray Robinson Story* (Copyright © 1969, 1970 by Sugar Ray Robinson), Ronald K. Fried's *Corner Men*, Robert Cromie's "Life Story of the Man Who Beat Louis" (17 October 1950), Donald Dewey's *Ray Arcel: A Boxing Biography* (Copyright © 2012 by Donald Dewey), Robert Markus's "A Man Needs Help . . . His Name is Charles" in *Chicago Daily Tribune* (10 October 1968), "The Most Important Bout of Ezzard Charles" in *Ebony* (March 1969), "They're Just Names Now" by Phil Musick in *Pittsburgh Press* (9 February 1975), and "The Magnificent Loser" by Bob McKay in *Cincinnati Magazine* (October 1977) were used as resources for this essay.

"The Third God of War": The author is indebted to Cherie Burns's work in *The Great Hurricane: 1938* (Copyright © 2005 by Cherie Burns). Ronald K. Fried's *Corner Men*, Peter Heller's interviews of Henry Armstrong and Lou Ambers in *In This Corner*, Douglas Century's *Barney Ross*, *Sugar Ray* by Sugar Ray Robinson with Dave Anderson were resources. Whitey Bimstein made the comment about Lou Ambers being a "trainer's dream" and his only vice.

"The Second God of War": The author would like to acknowledge the work of Milton Gross, Jack Hand, and Arthur Daley, as well as *Sugar Ray* by Sugar Ray Robinson with Dave Anderson, Peter Heller's *In This Corner*, A.J. Liebling's *The Sweet Science* (Copyright © 1951, 1952, 1953, 1954, 1955, 1956 by A.J. Liebling) and Wil Haygood's biography *Sweet Thunder: The Life and Times of Sugar*

Ray Robinson (Copyright © 2009 by Wil Haygood). "The gods themselves . . ." is from Shakespeare's King Lear. Special thanks to Dr. John O'Neill of Nantucket.

"The God of War": *Battling Siki: A Tale of Ring Fixes, Race, and Murder in the 1920s* by Peter Benson (Copyright © 2006 by University of Arkansas Press) and *The Pussycat of Prizefighting: Tiger Flowers and the Politics of Black Celebrity* by Andrew M. Kaye. (Copyright © 2004 by the University of Georgia Press) were resources for this essay. I am indebted to Bill Paxton, author of the landmark biography *The Fearless Harry Greb: Biography of a Tragic Hero of Boxing* (Copyright © 2009 Bill Paxton), and to S.L. Compton, author of the definitive Greb biography *Live Fast, Die Young: The Life and Times of Harry Greb* (Copyright © 2006 by Stephen L. Compton). Special thanks to William H. Hooke.

"Out of the Past": Details about Johnny Wilson in 1970 from Bud Collins' "Portrait of an Ex-Champ" (*Boston Globe*, 15 November 1970); Jock Malone's dive off the Charlestown Bridge was reported by the *Boston Daily Globe* ("Malone Leaps 50 Feet Into The Harbor, Big Crowd Watching," 1 August 1924). DeMarco's ascension to the title is also reported by the *Boston Globe* ("DeMarco Wins Welter Crown; TKO Victor Over Saxton In 14th," 2 April 1955).

My publisher Harry Otty deserves a medal for his patience with this perfectionist. Thanks to boxing historian Alister Scott Ottesen and editors Michael Woods, Julie Cockerham, and Laura Carlson for their assistance. Dino da Vinci has earned my gratitude for proving to be one of the few stand-up guys in boxing. Finally, I want to thank my mother, Barbara Toledo, who taught my brother and me to open our hands and always look up.

Index